Lenten Prayer for Families

Lenten Prayer for Families

Colleen Pressprich

Illustrated by Amy Heyse

OSV

Our Sunday Visitor
Huntington, Indiana

For my godsons, Alexander and Thomas, with love. (C.P.)
To Kevin, Holly, and Mayumi. Together in Paris. Je vous aime. *(A.H.)*

Nihil Obstat
Msgr. Michael Heintz, Ph.D.
Censor Librorum

Imprimatur
✠ Kevin C. Rhoades
Bishop of Fort Wayne-South Bend
July 29, 2025

The *Nihil Obstat* and *Imprimatur* are official declarations that a book is free from doctrinal or moral error. It is not implied that those who have granted the *Nihil Obstat* and *Imprimatur* agree with the contents, opinions, or statements expressed.

Scripture texts in this work are taken from the *New Revised Standard Version Bible: Catholic Edition*, copyright © 1989, 1993 National Council of the Churches of Christ in the United States of America. Used by permission. All rights reserved worldwide.

Excerpts from the English translation of the *Catechism of the Catholic Church* for use in the United States of America Copyright © 1994, United States Catholic Conference, Inc.—Libreria Editrice Vaticana. Used with Permission. English translation of the *Catechism of the Catholic Church*: Modifications from the Editio Typica copyright © 1997, United States Conference of Catholic Bishops—Libreria Editrice Vaticana.

Every reasonable effort has been made to determine copyright holders of excerpted materials and to secure permissions as needed. If any copyrighted materials have been inadvertently used in this work without proper credit being given in one form or another, please notify Our Sunday Visitor in writing so that future printings of this work may be corrected accordingly.

Copyright © 2026 by Colleen Pressprich
Artwork copyright © 2026 by Our Sunday Visitor, Inc.

31 30 29 28 27 26   1 2 3 4 5 6 7 8 9

All rights reserved. With the exception of short excerpts for critical reviews, no part of this work may be reproduced or transmitted in any form or by any means whatsoever without permission from the publisher. For more information, visit: www.osv.com/permissions.

Our Sunday Visitor Publishing Division
Our Sunday Visitor, Inc., 200 Noll Plaza, Huntington, IN 46750; www.osv.com; 1-800-348-2440.

ISBN: 978-1-63966-336-1 (Inventory No. T2975)
1. RELIGION—Holidays—Easter & Lent.
2. JUVENILE NONFICTION—Holidays & Celebrations—Easter & Lent.
3. RELIGION—Christianity—Catholic.

eISBN: 978-1-63966-337-8

Cover and interior design: Amanda Falk
Cover and interior art: Colleen Pressprich

Printed by PrintCenter in Turkey

Contents

Introduction for Parents

Welcome to Lent, one of the most solemn seasons of the Church's liturgical year. During this season we are invited to go deeper, to renew our commitment to our faith, and to prepare our hearts for the gift of the Resurrection.

But how?

That's the question I get most often from other parents. They tell me that Advent is easier because there are traditions such as the Jesse Tree and the Advent wreath that help them anchor their family's prayer.

This book is my answer to that question, for my own family and for yours. Within these pages you'll find what you need to build a daily rhythm of prayer during this season of Lent.

WHAT IS LENT?

Lent is the liturgical season of preparation ahead of Easter — the Church's most sacred day. Lent begins on Ash Wednesday and ends on the evening of Holy Thursday. Throughout this season, Catholics around the world are encouraged to lean into prayer, fasting, and almsgiving, known as the three pillars of Lent. By doing so, we unite ourselves with Jesus during his forty days of temptation in the desert (see Matthew 4:1–11 for the account). We can think of these three pillars as the three legs of a stool. A stool cannot stand on only one leg, nor even two; it needs all three to be sturdy and operable. The same is true of Lent.

This book is meant to be a jumping-off point that helps you center your life more fully on Jesus during this holy season. Prayer, fasting, and almsgiving are interwoven throughout in the Scriptures chosen for each day, the meditations, and the notes for parents at the end of the book. My hope is that this book, while it most directly supports your family's prayer during this season, will help you find concrete ways to incorporate all three pillars into your Lent.

THIS BOOK'S CONTENT AND STRUCTURE

I cannot think of a better way to prepare hearts and minds for the joy of Easter than to spend Lent diving into the Living Word of God as a family, which is why Scripture is the heart of this devotional. The content of each day is made up of a Scripture passage, a short meditation, a prayer, and a few conversation starters to facilitate discussion with your children. If you want more information or guidance on any given day, you can consult the Notes for Parents section at the back of the book.

For the first few days, beginning on Ash Wednesday, each Scripture reading will come directly from the Mass. Once the First Sunday of Lent arrives, the content will shift to a week-by-week theme. Each week will also include a Scripture verse for memorization to help your family enter more deeply into the week's theme, pondering and praying even when you are not engaging with this book. Each of the weekly themes was chosen intentionally and prayerfully to allow your family to live the season of Lent more deeply, no matter the ages of your children or the stage of life in which you find yourself. The themes are:

- First Week of Lent: Conversion of Heart
- Second Week of Lent: Prayer
- Third Week of Lent: Repentance
- Fourth Week of Lent: Reconciliation
- Fifth Week of Lent: Renewal and Restoration

The Sixth Sunday of Lent is also Palm Sunday, which marks the beginning of Holy Week. Here the Scripture passages will switch back to being day-specific in order to help your family lean into the traditions and rituals of the Church.

If you've flipped ahead, you will have noticed that the book doesn't end on Easter Sunday. This is important because Easter is a feast that lasts for an octave (eight days). After a long Lenten preparation, we want to be sure that we feast for the full eight days of Easter, following along with Jesus after his resurrection!

SUGGESTIONS FOR USING THIS BOOK TO GO DEEPER THIS LENT

There are as many ways to use this book as there are families who will open it, and the structure of the book is designed to help you find what will work for you. With that in mind, here are a few suggestions to get you started.

First, prayer routines often work best when they are tied to an activity that your family already does. For example, in my family, dinnertime and bedtime are both points in our schedule where we can fit prayer with relative ease, because we are already gathering as a family, and my husband and I already have our kids' attention.

If you miss a day, don't worry. It happens! The length of the season of Lent makes it likely that you will miss a meditation here and there. When that happens, you can either double up two days' worth of meditations or simply skip the missed passage and move on. Do what works best for your family, and don't worry about doing this devotional "perfectly."

The way you approach this devotional will depend in large part on the ages of your children. If your children are still young, read the meditation and look at the pictures in one sitting. This can take as little as five minutes; though I often find my children are drawn to the illustrations, and if that's the case, I let them look as long as they are interested. Loop back to the conversation starters over dinner or on the car ride home from school. You may choose to try some of the ideas in the Notes for Parents section as applicable and interesting for your children.

If your children are in middle grades or older, incorporate some *lectio divina* into your prayer time. This can work in a few different ways. Maybe you all read the Scripture passage and meditation together, and then everyone spends ten minutes praying about it individually before you come back and discuss (this doesn't have to be a long discussion — maybe five to ten minutes). Or you might choose to use the conversation starters from the previous day to start the prayer session after everyone has had some time to think and pray about them.

A note on the conversation starters: They are designed to do just that: spark conversation with your kids about the Faith. Sometimes, it's tough to get our kids to open up, but a well-placed question can work wonders. That being said, you don't have to have these conversations right after the daily meditation. You can come back later in the day or even the next day. Also, it's OK not to do them at all if your family gets talking on a different aspect of the reading and has a fruitful discussion! The conversation starters are there to help you, not to obligate or make you feel guilty.

In addition to the daily reflections, each week we will highlight one verse from Scripture to memorize, to help deepen your prayer and meditation with the weekly theme. Why is this important? Memorization is an educational technique that was once at the center of schooling for young people. And while there are good reasons that pedagogy has evolved to include other ways of teaching, memorization remains an important tool in certain situations. We memorize important information: data we want at our fingertips, things that make our lives easier, like multiplication tables, addresses, and phone numbers, to name a few.

As Catholics, we should be adding Scripture to that list. If our children have Scripture passages memorized, the verses will be in their minds and on the tip of their tongues later in life, offering comfort, guidance, support, and peace even when they find themselves in difficult situations.

Here are some simple tips and tricks for memorizing the weekly Scripture verse as a family:

- Print out the verse and place it on the fridge and your bathroom mirrors. This way you and all of the readers in the family will see it multiple times a day.
- Practice the verse out loud when you get in the car or before you say grace at mealtimes.
- Make it a game. Create a Scripture style game of Popcorn, where one person begins the verse and then stops, calling on the next person to pick up the verse at the next word and continue.
- If you homeschool, Scripture memorization lends itself brilliantly to handwriting practice.

THE NOTES FOR PARENTS SECTION

This book includes a section of notes for parents at the end, with one "note" corresponding to each daily reflection. These notes are not meant to be read as part of the daily reflection with your children but are designed to encourage you and boost your confidence as your child's primary educator in the Faith. Within these notes, I've provided extra context for more obscure books of the Bible or traditions, and I have tried to anticipate common challenging questions kids ask. You'll also find suggestions for going deeper and concrete ideas for incorporating some of the important themes into your family's daily life.

As you prepare to dive into the season of Lent, my final piece of advice is to be kind to yourself. Lent is a marathon, not a sprint. There will be days when your Lenten prayer feels fruitful and deep, and days where you feel like you are white-knuckling through these meditations. God's mercy covers all, and the Lord bestows grace on all of our efforts. Sometimes the prayer that bears the most fruit is the prayer that feels the dryest in the moment.

I pray that you and your family have a blessed Lent.

Ash Wednesday

Yet even now says the Lord,
return to me with all your heart,
with fasting, with weeping, and with mourning;
rend your hearts and not your clothing.
Return to the Lord, *your God,*
for he is gracious and merciful,
slow to anger, and abounding in steadfast love,
and relents from punishing. (Joel 2:12–13)

These verses from the prophet Joel remind us of three important truths: First, God wants our whole self, not just a part of us. Wherever our relationship with him is right now, he is hoping for more this Lent. Secondly, our God is a God of love and mercy. He asks us to return to him not so he can punish or berate us, but so he can help us, heal us, and love us. Third, we are not meant to take this journey of Lent alone; everyone is called to participate and to work together along the way.

Whether this is your first Lent or your fifty-first, God has plans for you this year. Returning to him is just the first step.

PRAYER

Dear Lord, as we begin our Lenten journey, help us to enter into this season with our whole hearts. May we experience your mercy and love in a new and deeper way this Lent, both as individuals and as a family. Amen.

Conversation Starters

- What would it look like for you to return to God with your whole heart?
- This Lent, how can your family or community support you in returning to God? Are there ways you could be encouraging to others this Lent?
- Would you like to share your Lenten sacrifice or penance? Why did you choose it?

Thursday After Ash Wednesday

Have mercy on me, O God,
according to your steadfast love;
according to your abundant mercy
blot out my transgressions.
Wash me thoroughly from my iniquity,
and cleanse me from my sin.

Create in me a clean heart, O God,
and put a new and right spirit within me.
Do not cast me away from your presence,
and do not take your holy spirit from me.
Restore to me the joy of your salvation,
and sustain in me a willing spirit.
(*Psalm* 51:1–2, 10–12)

King David, the writer of many of the psalms, was a man who knew his own weaknesses well. But he also had a bone-deep knowledge of the Lord's goodness, which meant he was never afraid to acknowledge his struggles or to ask for help with them. In Psalm 51, he asks God for many things. He wants healing. He wants restoration of joy. He wants wisdom. He wants his sins to be blotted out. None of these requests from David are small items. And yet he makes them with confidence because he knows this truth about God: God will never turn away those who are sorry for the wrong they have done.

PRAYER

God, please help us to keep our eyes fixed on you this Lent. May we praise you and rejoice in this time of penance and sacrifice because we know that it will bring us closer to you. Amen.

Conversation Starters

- This psalm is full of descriptive verbs and powerful adjectives. Did any words stand out to you when we read it? Why?
- Do you feel confident enough in God to make big requests of him? Why?

Friday After Ash Wednesday

"When you give alms, do not let your left hand know what your right hand is doing, so that your alms may be done in secret; and your Father who sees in secret will reward you. Whenever you pray, go into your room and shut the door and pray to your Father who is in secret; and your Father who sees in secret will reward you. When you are praying, do not heap up empty phrases as the Gentiles do; for they think that they will be heard because of their many words. Do not be like them, for your Father knows what you need before you ask him." (Matthew 6:3–4, 6–8)

This passage offers us so much hope! We don't need to worry about being perfect, looking right, or having fancy words to pray with. We don't have to prove to God that we are worth listening to. God hears our prayers because he is a Father who loves us and knows what we need. We can bring our honest, authentic, vulnerable selves to God. Isn't that a relief? Lent is a wonderful time to practice being honest and vulnerable with God and our family. It can even be a part of our Lenten penance!

PRAYER

Dear Jesus, please help us to remember that you know and love all parts of us. Help us to be more authentic in our prayers this Lent. Amen.

Conversation Starters

- Why do you think Jesus needed to remind the people to give alms and pray in secret?
- Everyone prays differently. Some people prefer to pray in a church, other people in their bedrooms. Some people prefer to listen to music, and others enjoy having a piece of art to look at while they pray. What things help you during your prayer time? Are there any methods you'd like to try?

Saturday after Ash Wednesday

Therefore you have no excuse, whoever you are, when you judge others; for in passing judgment on another you condemn yourself, because you, the judge, are doing the very same things. You say, "We know that God's judgment on those who do such things is in accordance with truth." Do you imagine, whoever you are, that when you judge those who do such things and yet do them yourself, you will escape the judgment of God? Or do you despise the riches of his kindness and forbearance and patience? Do you not realize that God's kindness is meant to lead you to repentance? (Romans 2:1–4)

It's easy to get into the habit of judging others. Our culture often encourages us to sort people into groups and then label and judge those groups. We divide ourselves by appearance, favorite activity, opinions, and many other things. Two thousand years ago, the Christian community in Rome fell into this same habit. They divided themselves into two groups: those who had been Jews before their conversion and those who had been Gentiles (everyone else). There were lots of arguments about which group was better and which group God loved more. Here's what they forgot: God loved them both. It didn't matter to him which group they fell into because God doesn't play favorites.

We have been given so much. We have been blessed beyond all measure. We have been brought into the family of God. Lent gives us the chance to remember and be thankful for God's kindness, mercy, and patience with us and to allow his love to lead us to repentance.

Conversation Starters

- What are some ways that you notice people being judged? In what ways do you judge others?
- What are some ways you can better focus on God's kindness to you?

PRAYER

Dear Lord, please help us to stop judging those around us, and to remember that you love all your children. Help us to see the good in everyone we encounter this Lent, especially those in our own family. Amen.

Week One:

Conversion of Heart

This week we'll be reading and praying with Scripture passages that focus on conversion of heart. At its simplest, conversion of heart is turning back toward the Lord. It's often a process that happens little by little, with many small steps and consistent prayers.

We'll be looking at a different passage from the Bible each day this week to see what it can show us about what it means to have a conversion of heart.

Weekly Memorization Verse

Your word is a lamp to my feet
and a light to my path. (Psalm 119:105)

First Sunday of Lent

Your word is a lamp to my feet
and a light to my path.
I have sworn an oath and confirmed it,
to observe your righteous ordinances.
Your decrees are my heritage forever;
they are the joy of my heart.
I incline my heart to perform your statutes
forever, to the end. (Psalm 119:105–106, 111–112)

It's difficult to take a walk in the dark, even if it's just across your backyard. Without a light, you're likely to trip on a stick or a toy, run into a piece of furniture, or hit your head on a low-hanging branch. But with a flashlight, that same walk is much easier, isn't it? This is also true in our spiritual lives. God's law is the light to our path. Sometimes we think of God's law as a list of things we can't do. But God's law wasn't just written to tell us what actions to avoid; it was written to protect us from the things that could harm us. Just like a flashlight on a dark walk, the law illuminates the dangers in the world. Most importantly, it was designed to help us know who God is and how deeply he loves us. If we spend time with God's Word, it will light our way and keep us close to him.

Conversation Starters

- Have you ever tried to walk in the dark? What was that experience like? How did you feel?
- Have you ever experienced God's law as a kind of light in your life? What was that like?

PRAYER

Dear Lord, please help us to spend more time with Scripture this Lent. Help us to understand it, to appreciate its wisdom, and to love you more as it helps us to know you better. Amen.

Monday of the First Week of Lent

At that time the disciples came to Jesus and asked, "Who is the greatest in the kingdom of heaven?" He called a child, whom he put among them, and said, "Truly I tell you, unless you change and become like children, you will never enter the kingdom of heaven. Whoever becomes humble like this child is the greatest in the kingdom of heaven. Whoever welcomes one such child in my name welcomes me. (Matthew 18:1–5)

Have you ever watched toddlers jump into a pool into their father's arms? Even if they don't know how to swim, they'll still launch themselves into the water with full confidence that their dad will catch them. Most of the time, young kids don't even think before they jump; they don't worry about whether they've behaved well enough for Dad to catch them, and they don't wonder what will happen if he doesn't. They just know that their father loves them and he's there.

When Jesus tells his disciples to become like children, he's telling them that they need to have that level of trust in God. Sometimes as we get older, we forget how to trust God as our Father. We forget that we can and should launch ourselves into his arms, ready to tell him everything that's happened to us, the good and the bad, fully expecting him to keep us safe. It doesn't matter how we've behaved. It doesn't matter if we forgot to pray yesterday or the day before. God loves us and will be with us.

PRAYER

Dear Lord, help us to trust you more today than we did yesterday. Help us to remember that we are your children and that you love us unconditionally. Amen.

Conversation Starters

- Have you ever jumped into a pool into your parents' arms? How did you feel when they caught you?
- Can you imagine being caught like that by God?
- Do you ever have a hard time trusting God? In what ways?
- What might help you to trust more deeply in God?
- What might change in your life if you became more childlike in your trust?

Tuesday of the First Week of Lent

I appeal to you therefore, brothers and sisters, by the mercies of God, to present your bodies as a living sacrifice, holy and acceptable to God, which is your spiritual worship. Do not be conformed to this world, but be transformed by the renewing of your minds, so that you may discern what is the will of God — what is good and acceptable and perfect. (Romans 12:1–2)

Have you ever tried to find something in the dark? Even if you know the item is in the room, it's much harder to find it without a light. This is true of discernment is as well. To discern something means to recognize it, to distinguish it from other choices and options. The most important thing for us to discern is God's will: what he wants us to do.

When we listen to God's word and pay attention to it, by spending time in prayer and reading Scripture, we are better able to understand his will, and to follow it, even when it's hard.

Remember Jesus' prayer in the Garden of Gethsemane before he was crucified? He prayed that God's will would be done, even though it was scary, and even though he knew it was going to be painful and difficult.

PRAYER

Dear Lord, please help us to stay close to your heart and to discern your will correctly in our lives, even when it's difficult. Amen.

Conversation Starters

- When we discern something, we figure it out. What tools do you have to help you discern God's will (even when it's difficult or scary)? What tools do you need?
- What are some ways you are staying close to God this Lent? What help or encouragement might help you with that?

Wednesday of the First Week of Lent

My soul thirsts for God,
for the living God.
When shall I come and behold
the face of God?
My tears have been my food
day and night,
while people say to me continually,
"Where is your God?"

Why are you cast down, O my soul,
and why are you disquieted
within me?

Hope in God; for I shall again praise
him,
my help and my God.

My soul is cast down within me;
therefore I remember you
from the land of Jordan and of
Hermon,
from Mount Mizar.
(Psalm 42:2–3, 5–6)

Can you remember a time when you were really, really thirsty? When we're thirsty, it's hard to think about anything other than finding a drink. The thought of water consumes us, and nothing else matters. That's the feeling this psalm describes. What would it feel like to thirst for God as much as you do for water on a hot day? What would you do to satisfy your need for God?

In the Gospel of John, Jesus meets a woman at the well who has not been leading a virtuous life. He tells her that he is the living water that quenches our deepest thirst. God wants us all to know that he made us for himself, and our souls are thirsty until we find him! As Catholics, we have many opportunities to encounter God. We can attend daily Mass, go to Eucharistic adoration, or simply stop by our local parish and visit Jesus in the tabernacle. We can read the Bible, listen to worship music, or pray the Rosary. Today let's ask God to help us thirst for him so we will always look to him alone to satisfy us.

Conversation Starters

- When was a time that you were very thirsty? What did you do? How did you feel when that thirst was satisfied?
- Do you thirst for God? What does that feel like?

PRAYER

Dear Lord, please fill us with your Holy Spirit and help us to thirst and hunger for you more deeply. Amen.

Thursday of the First Week of Lent

Submit yourselves therefore to God. Resist the devil, and he will flee from you. Draw near to God, and he will draw near to you. Cleanse your hands, you sinners, and purify your hearts, you double-minded. Lament and mourn and weep. Let your laughter be turned into mourning and your joy into dejection. Humble yourselves before the Lord, and he will exalt you. (James 4:7–10)

We need to humble ourselves before the Lord. But what does it mean to be humble, and why should we do it before God? The word *humble* is one of the most misunderstood in the English language. Many people believe that being humble means looking down on yourself or playing down your skills and talents so that they seem less than they are. But that's not true humility. True humility means having an honest opinion of ourselves, regarding both our strengths and our weaknesses. If we are humble, we see ourselves clearly, as God sees us.

This can be hard to do — in part, because the devil doesn't want us to do it. He hates humility, because it leads us closer to God. Growing in humility helps us to resist the devil, just as Jesus did when he was tempted in the desert. When we see ourselves as we really are and bring our true selves to God, he can do two things in our lives: He can add his strength to the places where we are weak, and he can refine and help us to develop our strengths and talents. In this way, he will raise us up to be better, fuller versions of ourselves.

Conversation Starters

- What are some strengths that you have? What are some of your weaknesses?
- How can you bring these to God with honesty?

PRAYER

Dear Jesus, please help us to be honest about our struggles and our strengths. Help us to be willing to lean on your grace for strength in our weakness and to shine in the talents you have given us. Amen.

Friday of the First Week of Lent

Wash yourselves; make
yourselves clean;
remove the evil of your doings
from before my eyes;
cease to do evil,
learn to do good;
seek justice,
rescue the oppressed,
defend the orphan,
plead for the widow.

Come now, let us argue it out,
says the L*ORD*:
though your sins are like scarlet,
they shall be like snow;
though they are red like crimson,
they shall become like wool.
(Isaiah 1:16–18)

If you've ever tried to get a permanent marker stain off a shirt (or a wall), you know how difficult it can be. Most of the time, even after a lot of scrubbing and elbow grease, the best result still shows a hint of what used to be there. That's because once something is stained, be it fabric or a wall, it's almost impossible to return it to its original state. And that's how it can feel sometimes with sin, isn't it? Especially with sins that have become habitual, it can feel like even though we've confessed them, even though we are working at removing them from our lives, a trace of them always seems to remain.

Yet this passage from Isaiah tells us that isn't true. With his sweat and blood, Jesus removed the entire stain of sin for us. When Isaiah shared this prophecy with the Israelites, they could only wait in hope for a time when their sins would be forgiven. But we have that opportunity right now — as often as we want or need — in the Sacrament of Reconciliation. Let's not take that gift for granted; it came at a tremendous cost.

Conversation Starters

- What questions do you have about the Sacrament of Reconciliation?
- How do you feel knowing that God can completely free you from your sins?

PRAYER

Dear Jesus, thank you for the Sacrament of Reconciliation. Thank you for the grace that you pour out on us. Thank you for being fully present to us in each of the sacraments we receive. Help us to understand the meaning of these sacraments and to appreciate them more deeply. Amen.

Saturday of the First Week of Lent

For surely I know the plans I have for you, says the L*ORD*, *plans for your welfare and not for harm, to give you a future with hope. Then when you call upon me and come and pray to me, I will hear you. When you search for me, you will find me; if you seek me with all your heart, I will let you find me, says the* L*ORD*, *and I will restore your fortunes and gather you from all the nations and all the places where I have driven you, says the* L*ORD*, *and I will bring you back to the place from which I sent you into exile. (Jeremiah 29:11–14)*

Let this passage from Jeremiah wash over you and remind you of just how precious you are to the Lord. God, in his infinite wisdom and mercy and love, has made plans for *you*, as an individual. He planned to send his Son to save his people, and that includes you. That's a truth worth holding on to, especially during the rigors of Lent. We encounter many *whats* and *hows* and *shoulds* during Lent, but this passage explains the *why*. Conversion of heart matters because it opens us up to experience the plans that God has for us. It ensures that we will be able to recognize and cherish those good things.

Conversation Starters

- How did you feel when you heard this passage? What thoughts came to mind?
- What do you think is God's plan for you? Why?

PRAYER

Thank you, Lord, for the gift of your love. Thank you for knowing, loving, and planning for each one of us — as individuals and as a family. Please help us hold onto your love when we are tempted or when our prayer feels stale. Amen.

Week Two:

Prayer

This week we'll be reading Scripture passages that focus on prayer: what it is and how to do it, and how it changes our hearts. There are many types of prayer and many ways of lifting our hearts to God.

Weekly Memorization Verse

Do not worry about anything, but in everything by prayer and supplication with thanksgiving let your requests be made known to God. (Philippians 4:6)

Second Sunday of Lent

Pray then in this way:
Our Father in heaven,
hallowed be your name.
Your kingdom come.
Your will be done,
on earth as it is in heaven.
Give us this day our daily bread.
And forgive us our debts,
as we also have forgiven our debtors.
And do not bring us to the time of trial,
but rescue us from the evil one. (Matthew 6:9–13)

This is one of those passages that is easy to skim over because it's so familiar to us that we think, "Oh, I know this already." Yet the reality is that the Bible contains the Living Word of God, and it can always speak to our hearts in new ways if we let it. Don't take the words of the Lord's Prayer for granted. Instead, pause. Ask the Holy Spirit to help you pray them well. Remember that Jesus himself gave us these words to pray.

He gave them for you — not just for everyone generally, but for *you*, right here and right now. These words are purposeful. They are powerful.

Read the passage again, this time imagining Jesus in front of you.

PRAYER

Dear Jesus, help us to always approach your word with open hearts. Help us to always be attentive to what you might be trying to tell us. Amen.

Conversation Starters

- Did anything new stand out to you the second time we read this passage? If so, what stood out?
- Why do you think Jesus chose these particular words when his apostles asked him to teach them how to pray?

Monday of the Second Week of Lent

Rejoice in the Lord always; again I will say, Rejoice. Let your gentleness be known to everyone. The Lord is near. Do not worry about anything, but in everything by prayer and supplication with thanksgiving let your requests be made known to God. And the peace of God, which surpasses all understanding, will guard your hearts and your minds in Christ Jesus. (Philippians 4:4–7)

Why do we have to ask God to give us what we need when he already knows everything? It seems like a reasonable question to ask, and yet, this passage makes it very clear that we should ask the Lord for everything — the little things as well as the big things.

Here's why: Our God is a God of relationships. We don't pray to him to inform him of things. Again, he knows everything already, including the things we want! But he wants us to tell him everything because he wants the opportunity to respond to us. He wants to grow our relationship with him.

Yes, God knows what we need before we ask. Yes, he will provide for us — often, even when we don't ask. But when we bring him our needs in prayer, we invite him into our lives. We use our free will to give him permission to respond.

Conversation Starters

- How do you share your everyday life with God? What have you found that works for you?
- How do you feel knowing that God wants to hear your voice and listen to you talk about your day? How does it feel to know that he wants to respond to you with love?

PRAYER

Dear God, thank you for loving us so much that you want to hear what we have to say. Help us to remember that we can always stop to talk with you whenever we need or want. Amen.

Tuesday of the Second Week of Lent

Therefore take up the whole armor of God, so that you may be able to withstand on that evil day, and having done everything, to stand firm. Stand therefore, and fasten the belt of truth around your waist, and put on the breastplate of righteousness. As shoes for your feet put on whatever will make you ready to proclaim the gospel of peace. With all of these, take the shield of faith, with which you will be able to quench all the flaming arrows of the evil one. Take the helmet of salvation, and the sword of the Spirit, which is the word of God. Pray in the Spirit at all times in every prayer and supplication. To that end keep alert and always persevere in supplication for all the saints. (Ephesians 6:13–18)

The armor of God described in this passage is incredibly powerful, but it's not like other armor. It isn't there to help us fight physical battles or attack those around us. The armor of God is meant to help us pray in the Spirit. But what does that mean? When we pray in the Spirit we are praying with the mind and heart of the Lord. We are seeking and desiring his will (not our own) for our lives and the lives of others. The armor of God defends us in times of temptation and keeps our souls safe from the attacks of the devil.

PRAYER

Dear Lord Jesus, please help us to put on the armor of God. Please send us your Holy Spirit so that we might be able to be truthful, faithful, and righteous. Amen.

Conversation Starters

- What elements of the armor of God stand out to you most? How can you "put them on" in your daily life?
- Why do you think Saint Paul wrote this passage of encouragement to the Church in Ephesus? What do you think they were struggling with?

Wednesday of the Second Week of Lent

So we have known and believe the love that God has for us.

God is love, and those who abide in love abide in God, and God abides in them. Love has been perfected among us in this: that we may have boldness on the day of judgment, because as he is, so are we in this world. There is no fear in love, but perfect love casts out fear; for fear has to do with punishment, and whoever fears has not reached perfection in love. We love because he first loved us. Those who say, "I love God," and hate their brothers or sisters, are liars; for those who do not love a brother or sister whom they have seen, cannot love God whom they have not seen. (1 John 4:16–20)

The perfect love that Saint John talks about in this passage is not a goal to strive for. It's a person. Jesus is perfect Love incarnate.

Understanding this truth helps us remember that because Jesus has come among us to abide with us, we can be bold; God remains in us. Some translations of this passage use the word *abide*, which implies more than just staying, but enduring. We know even within our own families that sometimes living with other people isn't easy. Sometimes it means that we have to tolerate or endure one another.

Saint John is talking about that, too. God endures us. And while that might sound a bit depressing, it is really very hopeful. God endures, God abides — not just in our shining moments but also in our darkest ones, those moments when we aren't so lovable, kind, or trustworthy. He loves us that much.

Conversation Starters

- How does it feel to think of Jesus being with you in all your best moments? What about your worst ones?
- What do you think it means when Saint John says, "Perfect love casts out fear"?

PRAYER

Thank you, Jesus, for loving us enough to abide with us. Thank you for not leaving us even when we are grumpy, angry, or struggling. Please help us this Lent to appreciate the gift of your presence with us more each day. Amen.

Thursday of the Second Week of Lent

O give thanks to the Lord, call on his name,
make known his deeds among the peoples.
Sing to him, sing praises to him,
tell of all his wonderful works.
Glory in his holy name;
let the hearts of those who seek the Lord rejoice.
Seek the Lord and his strength,
seek his presence continually. (1 Chronicles 16:8–11)

Can you imagine having a friend whom you only called when you were having a bad day? Probably not; right?

That's the point King David is trying to make in this passage. Like us, the Israelites were very good at reaching out to God when they needed help. But also like us, they often forgot to talk to him when things were going well. David wanted to make sure that his people remembered that they needed God all the time and that God wanted to be present and rejoice with them in the good moments as well as to help them in the bad ones.

PRAYER

Dear God, thank you for loving us enough to show up in our hard times. Help us to remember that you want to celebrate the good times with us as well. Help us to remember that we need your presence and your strength in every moment of our lives. Amen.

Conversation Starters

- Do you have a friend who is always there when you need something? What does that mean to you?
- What are some ways that you can remember to invite God into the everyday moments of your life?
- What are some ways that you can sing God's praises or glory in his holy name?

Friday of the Second Week of Lent

I said, "O Lord God of heaven, the great and awesome God who keeps covenant and steadfast love with those who love him and keep his commandments; let your ear be attentive and your eyes open to hear the prayer of your servant that I now pray before you day and night for your servants, the people of Israel, confessing the sins of the people of Israel, which we have sinned against you. O Lord, let your ear be attentive to the prayer of your servant, and to the prayer of your servants who delight in revering your name. Give success to your servant today, and grant him mercy in the sight of this man!" (Nehemiah 1:5–6, 11)

Nehemiah was a great political leader of Judah. A man of action, he is best known for rebuilding the walls of Jerusalem and taking steps to improve the lives of the people living there during a particularly difficult time in the history of the Israelites.

Nehemiah's accomplishments were significant, yet this passage shows that he understood the most important thing: Prayer had to come first. There are many things that we "do" as Catholics during Lent, but nothing is more important than honest and authentic prayer. Like Nehemiah, we need to orient ourselves correctly.

Conversation Starters

- What are some of the adjectives Nehemiah uses to describe God in his prayer? What do they tell us about the relationship he had with the Lord?
- What would you have done if you had been in Nehemiah's shoes?

PRAYER

Dear Lord, help us to turn to you as quickly and as honestly as Nehemiah did. Please help us not to hold anything back from you and to trust you completely with our needs. We entrust to you our Lent and ask that you guide our every step during this important season. Amen.

Saturday of the Second Week of Lent

Come and hear, all you who fear God,
and I will tell what he has done for me.
I cried aloud to him,
and he was extolled with my tongue.
If I had cherished iniquity in my heart,
the Lord would not have listened.
But truly God has listened;
he has given heed to the words of my prayer.
Blessed be God,
because he has not rejected my prayer
or removed his steadfast love from me.

(Psalm 66:16–20)

Sometimes, people misinterpret this psalm. They forget that listening isn't the same as saying yes. God will not always say yes to our prayers. In fact, most of us will experience many nos throughout our lives, for many different reasons.

But before he responds with a yes or a no, God always, always listens. He is steadfast. His love cannot be shaken or moved or diminished by our behavior.

He listens to understand. He listens to give aid. He listens to offer advice and encouragement. And sometimes, when our prayers are in line with his perfect will for our life, with what is best for us, he says yes and moves mountains to grant the desires of our hearts.

Conversation Starters

- What do you think King David was going through when he wrote this psalm? How do you think he was feeling?
- How do you feel when you reflect on this psalm?

PRAYER

Thank you, Lord, for loving us enough to listen to us. Thank you, Lord, for your unending, steadfast love for us. Help us to be open to all the ways that you respond to our prayers, instead of focusing only on whether you say yes or no. Amen.

Week Three:

Repentance

We're just about at the halfway point in our Lenten journey, and this week we'll be reading scripture passages about repentance. When we repent, we show through our words and our actions our sincere remorse for the wrong we have done.

Weekly Memorization Verse

For as the rain and snow come down from heaven,
and do not return there until they
have watered the earth,
making it bring forth and sprout,
giving seed to the sower and bread to the eater,
so shall my word be that goes out from my mouth;
it shall not return to me empty,
but it shall accomplish that which I purpose,
and succeed in the thing for which
I sent it. (Isaiah 55:10–11)

Third Sunday of Lent

In those days John the Baptist appeared in the wilderness of Judea, proclaiming, "Repent, for the kingdom of heaven has come near." When he saw many Pharisees and Sadducees coming for baptism, he said to them, "You brood of vipers! Who warned you to flee from the wrath to come? Bear fruit worthy of repentance. Even now the ax is lying at the root of the trees; every tree therefore that does not bear good fruit is cut down and thrown into the fire. I baptize you with water for repentance, but one who is more powerful than I is coming after me. I am not worthy to carry his sandals. He will baptize you with the Holy Spirit and fire." (Matthew 3:1–2, 6–8, 10–11)

Ouch. John the Baptist isn't pulling any punches in this passage. The people he is speaking to, the Pharisees and Sadducees, were leaders in the Jewish faith. These were men who knew God's commandments, who followed the law and were held in high esteem in Jewish society. But they also took the Lord for granted. Their lives had stopped bearing good fruit because they forgot that the law and the Commandments were there to help them know and love the Lord.

John's reminder to the Pharisees and Sadducees is a reminder for us, too. We have been given more than they had, for we have the sacraments (especially the Eucharist) and the ability to know and be in a loving relationship with God. Yet we can still forget to be grateful, forget to appreciate the blessings, forget that we should not take God for granted.

Conversation Starters

- Are there any things about being a Catholic that you take for granted? What do you think you could do to remember to appreciate those things more?
- Can you remember a time when you felt truly grateful for the blessings in your life? What did that feel like?

PRAYER

Dear Lord, please forgive us for the times and the ways that we have taken you for granted. Help us to appreciate all that you have given us, especially in our Catholic faith, and give us the grace to love you more deeply this Lent. Amen.

Monday of the Third Week of Lent

For as the rain and snow come down from heaven
and do not return there until they have watered
the earth,
making it bring forth and sprout,
giving seed to the sower and bread to the eater,
so shall my word be that goes out from my mouth;
it shall not return to me empty,
but it shall accomplish that which I purpose,
and succeed in the thing for which I sent it.
(Isaiah 55:10–11)

If you've ever learned about the water cycle in school, you know that the prophet Isaiah is correct in his description in this passage. When water falls to the earth as rain or snow, it is absorbed into the ground or collects and pools in lakes, streams, or oceans. But the water never stays exactly where it falls. It always does something, whether that is watering crops, quenching thirst, or cooling the earth. What's more, every droplet returns to the cycle eventually.

How long "eventually" is depends entirely on where that drop of water lands. A drop of water that lands on a hot sidewalk is going to evaporate pretty quickly. It might be a few years before a drop that lands in the ocean evaporates, and millennia before water that becomes part of a glacier returns to the atmosphere.

That's really important to keep in mind as we think about God's Word. Like the water cycle, God's word always accomplishes its purpose. But we don't always know what that purpose is, how he'll accomplish it, or what his timeline is.

Conversation Starters

- Just like there is always water moving through the water cycle, there is always grace being poured out onto you. What are the graces God is raining down on you right now?
- How does it feel to know that God's word always achieves the end for which he sent it?

PRAYER

Dear Lord, thank you for your word, which always accomplishes its purpose. Thank you for your plans, which are beyond our imagination. Please help us this Lent to remember that even though we don't always understand how you are working, we can be confident that you are. Amen.

Tuesday of the Third Week of Lent

Now I rejoice, not because you were grieved, but because your grief led to repentance; for you felt a godly grief, so that you were not harmed in any way by us. For godly grief produces a repentance that leads to salvation and brings no regret, but worldly grief produces death. For see what earnestness this godly grief has produced in you, what eagerness to clear yourselves, what indignation, what alarm, what longing, what zeal, what punishment! At every point you have proved yourselves guiltless in the matter. (2 Corinthians 7:9–11)

Even though the words are often used interchangeably, there is a difference between *hurt* and *harm*. This is why Saint Paul can tell the Corinthians that he rejoices over their grief. How can this be a good thing?

Take, for example, a cavity in your tooth. Getting your cavity filled will make your tooth healthy and strong again, but it won't be a comfortable process. It will probably hurt a little bit, but it definitely won't harm you. On the other hand, while that cavity was forming in your tooth, it likely didn't hurt at all. But if you leave it alone, it will harm you (and it will start to hurt, too). Untreated cavities can lead to all sorts of problems.

Sin is like a cavity. When we sin we are always harming ourselves, but sin doesn't always hurt in the moment. If left untreated, however, sin will lead to all sorts of problems. Repenting of our sins by going to confession and making changes in our lives so we don't sin again can be an uncomfortable process. It might hurt in the moment, but it does not harm us. On the contrary, it makes our soul healthy and strong.

Conversation Starters

- Have you ever had a cavity? What was it like for you to get it filled? How did you feel afterward?
- Just as we brush and floss our teeth to prevent cavities, there are things we can do to prevent sin from entering our lives. What things can you think of?
- Are there any areas of your life right now that are like a cavity that needs to be filled? What can you do to fix them?

PRAYER

Dear Jesus, please help us to see the areas in our lives where sin is harming us, even if we don't feel the hurt. May we have the strength and courage to confess our sins and follow you more fully this Lent. Amen.

Wednesday of the Third Week of Lent

Now all the tax collectors and sinners were coming near to listen to him. And the Pharisees and the scribes were grumbling and saying, "This fellow welcomes sinners and eats with them."

So he told them this parable: "Which one of you, having a hundred sheep and losing one of them, does not leave the ninety-nine in the wilderness and go after the one that is lost until he finds it? When he has found it, he lays it on his shoulders and rejoices. And when he comes home, he calls together his friends and neighbors, saying to them, 'Rejoice with me, for I have found my sheep that was lost.' Just so, I tell you, there will be more joy in heaven over one sinner who repents than over ninety-nine righteous persons who need no repentance." (Luke 15:1–7)

As we learned earlier this week, the Pharisees were leaders of the Jewish people who wanted to uphold God's law and his teachings, but they had forgotten about the importance of having a relationship with God. Though they were very careful to follow the rules of the Jewish religion, they were also very judgmental. One of the reasons they were angry with Jesus was because he spoke to and ate dinner with people they thought weren't worthy of time and attention.

It's important to hate sin *and* love sinners, which is why Jesus told the Pharisees this story about the lost sheep. He wanted them to remember that God loves all the people he created, not just those who are doing everything right or who look good by human standards. Jesus wanted them to remember that people can repent and turn back to God, but they need to have a relationship with him first. Jesus wants us to know that, too. Everyone is loved. Everyone is welcome.

Conversation Starters

- What do you think the Pharisees felt when they listened to the parable of the lost sheep?
- How do you think other people listening might have felt?
- Are there times you've felt like a Pharisee? What about a lost sheep?

PRAYER

Dear Jesus, help us to remember that you always love us, even when we stray far from you. Help us also to remember that you love the people around us. Remind us of their dignity and worth when we are tempted to judge them. Amen.

Thursday of the Third Week of Lent

The word of the Lord came to Jonah a second time, saying, "Get up, go to Nineveh, that great city, and proclaim to it the message that I tell you." So Jonah set out and went to Nineveh, according to the word of the Lord. Now Nineveh was an exceedingly large city, a three days' walk across. Jonah began to go into the city, going a day's walk. And he cried out, "Forty days more, and Nineveh shall be overthrown!" And the people of Nineveh believed God; they proclaimed a fast, and everyone, great and small, put on sackcloth.

When the news reached the king of Nineveh, he rose from his throne, removed his robe, covered himself with sackcloth, and sat in ashes.

When God saw what they did, how they turned from their evil ways, God changed his mind about the calamity that he had said he would bring upon them; and he did not do it. (Jonah 3:1–6, 10)

Nineveh was an important city belonging to a powerful empire. The people of Nineveh were not Jewish — in fact, they were enemies of the Jews — and yet God sent them one of his prophets. He cared about them even though they were sinning terribly, and as a result, their city was on the verge of destruction. When Jonah announced that news, the people of Nineveh did something unexpected: They believed God's word that their sin had real consequences. Their belief motivated them to take action, and the entire city turned away from sin.

It's easy to believe God's word and to follow him when his words to us are comforting or encouraging. It's a lot harder to do when he is asking us to make big, difficult changes to our lives. But when he points out our sin, he also offers us the grace to make changes.

Conversation Starters

- What do you think made the people of Nineveh believe Jonah's prophecy?
- What would you have done if you had been one of the Ninevites?

PRAYER

Dear Father, help us to be convicted like the people of Nineveh. May we recognize the sin in our lives and, like them, be moved to repentance. Amen.

Friday of the Third Week of Lent

And now, O Lord God of Israel, who brought your people out of the land of Egypt with a mighty hand and with signs and wonders and with great power and outstretched arm, and made yourself a name that continues to this day, we have sinned, we have been ungodly, we have done wrong, O Lord our God, against all your ordinances. Let your anger turn away from us, for we are left, few in number, among the nations where you have scattered us. Hear, O Lord, our prayer and our supplication, and for your own sake deliver us, and grant us favor in the sight of those who have carried us into exile; so that all the earth may know that you are the Lord our God, for Israel and his descendants are called by your name. (Baruch 2:11–15)

Even though Baruch is speaking to God in this passage, his words are also meant for the people of Israel who are listening to them. God's memory is perfect. God doesn't need to be reminded of the times that he has saved his people, and he doesn't need reminding that his people have sinned. But God's people do need to be reminded.

It's important for us to remember the things God has done in the past because it helps us stay faithful in the present. The people to whom Baruch was speaking had seen the Temple where they worshiped destroyed. They had suffered exile. They were beaten down and so focused on how bad things were that they had forgotten how much God loved them. Baruch reminds them and urges them to reclaim hope.

Conversation Starters

- What are some things that God has done for you in the past?
- When was a moment that you felt deeply loved by God?
- How can you record these good moments so they are easier to remember when you're having a hard time?

PRAYER

Lord, please help us to remember the blessings you have given us and the times you have saved us. Please send us your Holy Spirit so that we do not lose hope, especially in the midst of trials. Amen.

Saturday of the Third Week of Lent

To those who repent he grants a return,
and he encourages those who are losing hope.

Turn back to the Lord and forsake your sins;
pray in his presence and lessen your offense.

Return to the Most High and turn away from iniquity,
and hate intensely what he abhors.
How great is the mercy of the Lord,
and his forgiveness for those who return to him!
(Sirach 17:24–26, 29)

To have compassion for someone means to suffer with them. It's when we choose to let ourselves feel for and experience the pain of others.

Mercy goes a step beyond compassion. Mercy is when we see the misery of another person, realize that we have the power to change their situation, and act in a way that helps them instead of hurting them more or leaving them alone in their pain.

God is the best and truest example of mercy. As the all-powerful Creator, he is fully justified in punishing those who break his law. But in his mercy, God doesn't ever leave us alone in our sin, in our pain, or in our suffering. He always draws close to us. He always forgives us. He even sent his Son to die on the cross for us.

Mercy is at the very heart of who God is. And because we are created in the image and likeness of God, it is meant to be at the very heart of who we are as well.

Conversation Starters

- Who are some people you know (or know of) who might need mercy?
- What are some ways that you can be more merciful in your everyday life? How can your loved ones support you as you grow in mercy?

PRAYER

Dear Father, thank you for the mercy you show each of us. Thank you for the ways that you protect us and the times you have forgiven our sins. Please help us to grow in our understanding of mercy this Lent. Please remind us to show mercy to those around us. Amen.

Week Four:

Reconciliation

This week we'll be reading passages that focus on the theme of reconciliation. Reconciliation refers to the process of restoring good relations between people or groups. In this case, we're going to be focused on what it means to restore our relationship with God in the areas where we have broken it through our sin.

Weekly Memorization Verse

So when you are offering your gift at the altar, if you remember that your brother or sister has something against you, leave your gift there before the altar and go; first be reconciled to your brother or sister, and then come and offer your gift. (Matthew 5:23–24)

Fourth Sunday of Lent

For while we were still weak, at the right time Christ died for the ungodly. Indeed, rarely will anyone die for a righteous person — though perhaps for a good person someone might actually dare to die. But God proves his love for us in that while we still were sinners Christ died for us. Much more surely then, now that we have been justified by his blood, will we be saved through him from the wrath of God. For if while we were enemies, we were reconciled to God through the death of his Son, much more surely, having been reconciled, will we be saved by his life. But more than that, we even boast in God through our Lord Jesus Christ, through whom we have now received reconciliation. (Romans 5:6–11)

Think about your worst moment — the absolute lowest you have ever been, your very worst behavior, your greatest sin. Now remind yourself that at that exact moment in time, God loved you. God loved you then as much as he did at your best moment.

Sometimes we can slip into the belief that God won't believe us or receive us until we've earned his mercy. We promise ourselves, "I'll work on [this particular habit or sin], and then when I'm in better shape, I'll go back to prayer and confession." But that's not how God works.

We don't have to earn reconciliation with God. Because of his love and mercy, he is always ready to be reconciled with us. We should be running to God when we are at our lowest. He won't turn us away, no matter what sins we may have fallen into. He wants us to come at once.

Conversation Starters

- What do you think makes it hard to turn to God when we sin?
- How do you feel when you think about God seeing you and loving you in your worst moments?

PRAYER

Dear Jesus, thank you for loving us at our worst moments. Thank you for reminding us that we don't have to wait to be reconciled to you. Thank you for the ways that you are drawing us back to you this Lent. Please help us to run to you when we sin instead of staying away. Amen.

Monday of the Fourth Week of Lent

You have heard that it was said to those of ancient times, "You shall not murder"; and "whoever murders shall be liable to judgment." But I say to you that if you are angry with a brother or sister, you will be liable to judgment; and if you insult a brother or sister, you will be liable to the council; and if you say, "You fool," you will be liable to the hell of fire. So when you are offering your gift at the altar, if you remember that your brother or sister has something against you, leave your gift there before the altar and go; first be reconciled to your brother or sister, and then come and offer your gift. Come to terms quickly with your accuser while you are on the way to court with him, or your accuser may hand you over to the judge, and the judge to the guard, and you will be thrown into prison. Truly I tell you, you will never get out until you have paid the last penny. (Matthew 5:21–26)

Anger is an emotion that we all feel. It is not sinful to feel angry. Even Jesus felt anger, as we see in the Gospel accounts of Jesus overturning tables in the Temple. But Jesus teaches that we are responsible for what we do with our anger, no matter how someone else might have provoked it. If in our anger we lash out with hurtful words or deeds, it's our obligation to apologize and take responsibility for the part we have played in damaging our relationships with other people. We need to do this even if we didn't "start it" and even if the other person doesn't apologize.

PRAYER

Dear Jesus, please help us to do better at taking responsibility for how we respond when we are angry. Give us grace to help us pause and think about how you want us to treat other people even when are angry with them. Amen.

Conversation Starters

- Can you think of a time when someone apologized to you for a wrong they did you? How did you feel when the person apologized?
- Can you think of a time when you apologized to someone else for something you did wrong? How did you feel when you apologized?

Tuesday of the Fourth Week of Lent

So if anyone is in Christ, there is a new creation: everything old has passed away; see, everything has become new! All this is from God, who reconciled us to himself through Christ, and has given us the ministry of reconciliation; that is, in Christ God was reconciling the world to himself, not counting their trespasses against them, and entrusting the message of reconciliation to us. So we are ambassadors for Christ, since God is making his appeal through us; we entreat you on behalf of Christ, be reconciled to God. For our sake he made him to be sin who knew no sin, so that in him we might become the righteousness of God. (2 Corinthians 5:17–21)

An ambassador is an official representative of a king, queen, or government. Being an ambassador is an incredibly important job. Ambassadors speak on behalf of their entire country and promote the goals and values of that country when the king, queen, or other head of the government cannot be present.

You are an ambassador for Christ by virtue of your baptism. It is your job to bring Jesus' message to the people in your life — to tell them that Jesus loves them, that he died for their sins, and that no matter who they are or what they've done, they are valued and cherished by the God of the universe.

PRAYER

Dear Jesus, thank you for trusting us to be your ambassadors here on earth. Please help us share your love with others through our words and our actions. Amen.

Conversation Starters

- What are some concrete ways that you can be an ambassador for Christ in your daily life?
- What people in your life might need to hear that Jesus loves them and died for them?

Wednesday of the Fourth Week of Lent

He himself is before all things, and in him all things hold together. He is the head of the body, the church; he is the beginning, the firstborn from the dead, so that he might come to have first place in everything. For in him all the fullness of God was pleased to dwell, and through him God was pleased to reconcile to himself all things, whether on earth or in heaven, by making peace through the blood of his cross. (Colossians 1:17–20)

When Saint Paul wrote this letter, he was in prison. And yet he speaks of peace — a deep and abiding peace that is more than the absence of pain or conflict, a peace that can remain even in situations that cause distress.

Jesus died for our sins — for my sins and yours — so that he could present us to his Father. He wanted each of us to know his Father and be known by him for eternity. He died to bring us the peace that Saint Paul, writing from prison, talks about in this passage: peace through the blood of his cross. It's not a calm and quiet peace. It's not a peace that means the absence of pain or conflict, but rather a peace that remains even in situations of distress. This is the peace that God wants for us, the peace that Jesus died for.

Our job is to receive it.

Conversation Starters

- Saint Paul was in prison when he wrote this letter. Why do you think he wrote about peace the way he did?
- How does it feel to know that not only did Jesus die for you, but that he wants to bring you his Father?

PRAYER

Dear Jesus, thank you for reconciling all things to yourself. Thank you for making peace through the blood of your cross. Please open our hearts to receive your peace. Amen.

Thursday of the Fourth Week of Lent

So he set off and went to his father. But while he was still far off, his father saw him and was filled with compassion; he ran and put his arms around him and kissed him. Then the son said to him, "Father, I have sinned against heaven and before you; I am no longer worthy to be called your son." But the father said to his slaves, "Quickly, bring out a robe — the best one — and put it on him; put a ring on his finger and sandals on his feet. And get the fatted calf and kill it, and let us eat and celebrate; for this son of mine was dead and is alive again; he was lost and is found!" And they began to celebrate. (Luke 15:20–24)

The father in the parable doesn't wait for his estranged son to reach the house. He doesn't wait to hear the apology. He doesn't wait to learn why his son came home. He only cares that he did.

This is how God the Father behaves toward each one of us. No matter how far you have run from him or how long you've been away (from him or his Church), he will always run to greet you. He will always celebrate your return. He will always embrace you with full and complete love. He will always be overjoyed to have you home.

PRAYER

Heavenly Father, thank you for the warm welcome you give to us each and every time we return to you after we stray. Please help us to trust in your love. Amen.

Conversation Starters

- What do you think made the father run to his son instead of waiting? Were you surprised that the father wasn't angry? Why?
- How do you feel when you hear that God loves you like the father in this story loved his son?

Friday of the Fourth Week of Lent

But now in Christ Jesus you who once were far off have been brought near by the blood of Christ. For he is our peace; in his flesh he has made both groups into one and has broken down the dividing wall, that is, the hostility between us. He has abolished the law with its commandments and ordinances, that he might create in himself one new humanity in place of the two, thus making peace, and might reconcile both groups to God in one body through the cross, thus putting to death that hostility through it. So he came and proclaimed peace to you who were far off and peace to those who were near; for through him both of us have access in one Spirit to the Father. (Ephesians 2:13–18)

The kingdom of God includes all people. It's not just for the people who look a certain way or behave a certain way.

If you traveled across the world and attended Mass in a country where you didn't know the language or the culture, you would still know what to do. The Mass is the same everywhere: It contains the same readings, the same prayers, and the Consecration. But one of the beautiful things about the Catholic Church is that there are also differences. The architecture, the type of music, the clothes that people wear to church — these vary from place to place.

These differences are beautiful reminders that the kingdom of God is not just for some people; it belongs to all people.

Conversation Starters

- Have you ever heard the Mass celebrated in a language that wasn't your own? What was that like?
- What do you love about the Mass in your home parish?

PRAYER

Dear Jesus, thank you for the diversity in our Catholic Church. Please help us to remember that your kingdom belongs to everyone. Please open our eyes to the ways that we can be more welcoming and help us to appreciate the gifts and cultures of others. Amen.

Saturday of the Fourth Week of Lent

When it was evening on that day, the first day of the week, and the doors of the house where the disciples had met were locked for fear of the Jews, Jesus came and stood among them and said, "Peace be with you." After he said this, he showed them his hands and his side. Then the disciples rejoiced when they saw the Lord. Jesus said to them again, "Peace be with you. As the Father has sent me, so I send you." When he had said this, he breathed on them and said to them, "Receive the Holy Spirit. If you forgive the sins of any, they are forgiven them; if you retain the sins of any, they are retained." (John 20:19–23)

In this passage of his Gospel, Saint John describes the first time Jesus appeared to his apostles after his resurrection. Even though it happened on Easter, it's an important passage for Lent.

At the beginning of the passage, the apostles are scared. They fear for their lives, and that fear is valid. Then Jesus comes and breathes on them. With that breath, he bestows his peace, which changes them from the inside out. But in this visit, he also gives them a special gift, one that would change the world. He gives them his power to forgive sins, allowing us, two thousand years later, to experience the peace that comes with the breath of Jesus.

PRAYER

Dear Jesus, thank you for the Sacrament of Reconciliation. Please give us your grace to appreciate it and make use of it the way we should. Amen.

Conversation Starters

- How do you think the apostles felt when the Risen Christ appeared to them?
- Do you think the apostles were expecting Jesus to pass on to them his power to forgive sins? Why?

Week Five:

Renewal and Restoration

Today we begin the fifth week of our Lenten journey. This week we'll be praying with Scripture passages that focus on renewal and restoration. That means we'll be learning about what it means to let God repair parts of our lives and our relationship with him that have been broken.

Weekly Memorization Verse

"Come to me, all you that are weary and are carrying heavy burdens, and I will give you rest. Take my yoke upon you, and learn from me; for I am gentle and humble in heart, and you will find rest for your souls. For my yoke is easy, and my burden is light." (Matthew 11:28–30)

Fifth Sunday of Lent

The Lord, your God, is in your midst,
a warrior who gives victory;
he will rejoice over you with gladness,
he will renew you in his love;
he will exult over you with loud singing
as on a day of festival.
I will remove disaster from you,
so that you will not bear reproach for it. (Zephaniah 3:17–18)

The Lord God is in your midst, says the prophet Zephaniah, reminding the people of Jerusalem that they have a God unlike any other, a God who has stooped to dwell among his people, who wants to be with them. Even more than the Jewish people of Zephaniah's time, we know this to be true because of Jesus.

How often do we forget this reality? Too often, perhaps. And yet we have Jesus present in every tabernacle in the world. The Lord is in our midst. We can sit with him, spend time with him, be with him any time we wish. That is a tremendous gift we should not take for granted.

PRAYER

Dear Lord, thank you for loving us so much that you became bread and wine just to be close to us. Thank you for the gift of the Eucharist. Thank you for remaining present, Body and Blood, Soul and Divinity, in every tabernacle of the world. Amen.

Conversation Starters

- This passage describes several things God will do for his people. Which stood out to you? Why?
- What are some ways that you can remember that God is in your midst every day?

Monday of the Fifth Week of Lent

A new heart I will give you, and a new spirit I will put within you; and I will remove from your body the heart of stone and give you a heart of flesh. I will put my spirit within you, and make you follow my statutes and be careful to observe my ordinances. Then you shall live in the land that I gave to your ancestors; and you shall be my people, and I will be your God. (Ezekiel 36:26–28)

Six hundred years before Jesus was born, the Israelites, God's Chosen People, were living through a period that is known today as the Babylonian Exile. They had sinned by walking away from God and had stopped relying on him. As a consequence, they lost God's protection. The Temple in Jerusalem had been destroyed. Without it, they had nowhere to worship God and no way to keep his laws. The Temple had been their pride and joy, and now it was gone. The people who survived the destruction were deported and forced to leave their homeland and all they had known. It was a time of great pain and anguish.

In the midst of this, God sent the prophet Ezekiel to speak to his people. What a comfort these words must have been to them; what hope must have sprung up within each heart. God was going to give them his Spirit! He was going to provide for them and restore what had been lost.

Conversation Starters

- What do you think Ezekiel means when he says God is going to give his people a new heart? Why do you think they needed one?
- What examples can you think of that show how God has restored or renewed something that was broken or destroyed?

PRAYER

Thank you, Father, for reaching out to us when our hearts are cold. Thank you for restoring the broken parts of our lives and our hearts. Thank you for sending your Spirit to keep us close to you and help us follow your commandments. Amen.

Tuesday of the Fifth Week of Lent

> *Come to me, all you that are weary and are carrying heavy burdens, and I will give you rest. Take my yoke upon you, and learn from me; for I am gentle and humble in heart, and you will find rest for your souls. For my yoke is easy, and my burden is light. (Matthew 11:28–30)*

This Gospel passage gives us a decisive test to use to determine whether our labors and struggles are from the Lord or not. Jesus tells us that his yoke is easy and his burden is light. Does this mean that God won't ever ask us to do anything hard or that we won't struggle? No, of course not. Jesus tells us we will have to carry our crosses if we want to be his disciples (see Mt 16:24).

But sometimes we take on burdens that we aren't meant to carry. We might try to take on responsibilities or care for others in ways God isn't asking of us, even though we might have good intentions.

When Jesus says his yoke is easy and his burden is light, he doesn't mean that his followers will never have to suffer. What he does mean is that he'll always give us his strength and his grace to support us when we carry the burdens he allows and strive to do the work he has given us.

Conversation Starters

- Have you ever felt tired and burdened? What caused this?
- Can you think of a time when you took on a responsibility that wasn't yours? How did it go?

PRAYER

Dear Lord, thank you for your grace. Thank you for the ways that you support us. Thank you for reminding us to carry only what we are meant to. Help us to come to you when we are burdened. Amen.

Wednesday of the Fifth Week of Lent

One of the scribes came near and heard them disputing with one another, and seeing that he answered them well, he asked him, "Which commandment is the first of all?" Jesus answered, "The first is, 'Hear, O Israel: the Lord our God, the Lord is one; you shall love the Lord your God with all your heart, and with all your soul, and with all your mind, and with all your strength.' The second is this, 'You shall love your neighbor as yourself.' There is no other commandment greater than these." (Mark 12:28–31)

Saint Thérèse of Lisieux liked to compare souls to the flowers in a field or garden. She said, "Every flower has its own created beauty. The splendor of the rose, the lily's whiteness does not deprive the violet of its scent nor lessen the daisy's charm. … If every tiny flower wanted to be a rose, spring would lose its loveliness."

When we are ourselves — when we truly love the Lord with all of *our* heart, *our* soul, *our* mind, and *our* strength — we let God's light and love shine through us into the world. It doesn't matter if we are young or old, weak or strong, sick or healthy. We are not required or expected to be anything other than ourselves.

PRAYER

Dear Lord, thank you for the care you took in creating each one of us. Please help us to love you with all of our heart, soul, mind, and strength, not comparing ourselves to others or forgetting how much you love us. Amen.

Conversation Starters

- What's your favorite flower? What do you like about it?
- Do you ever compare yourself to others? What person (or people) have you compared yourself to? Why?
- Do you feel like you are loving God with your whole heart, soul, mind, and strength? How can your loved ones help support you in that?

Thursday of the Fifth Week of Lent

But when the goodness and loving kindness of God our Savior appeared, he saved us, not because of any works of righteousness that we had done, but according to his mercy, through the water of rebirth and renewal by the Holy Spirit. This Spirit he poured out on us richly through Jesus Christ our Savior, so that, having been justified by his grace, we might become heirs according to the hope of eternal life. (Titus 3:4–7)

God loves you intensely. He loves you passionately. He loves you beyond measure. He will always love you. You can't ever earn his love or deserve it, yet you have it wholeheartedly. God isn't stingy. He pours out his Spirit on us in abundance. He is extravagant.

Sometimes you will fail or fall or sin, and you will be tempted to turn away from the Lord because you are ashamed. When that happens, remember this passage. Remember that our God is a God of restoration and renewal. Our God is a God of unconditional love.

PRAYER

Dear God, thank you for your abundant love for us. Help us to remember your extravagant love in the times when we are tempted or struggling. Help us to turn to you when we are in need. Amen.

Conversation Starters

- Saint Paul tells us that God loves extravagantly. This means that he gives even more than is expected, a tremendous amount. What would it look like for you to love extravagantly?
- What do you think Saint Paul means that we have become "heirs" of eternal life?

Friday of the Fifth Week of Lent

Come, let us return to the Lord;
for it is he who has torn, and he will heal us;
he has struck down, and he will bind us up.
After two days he will revive us;
on the third day he will raise us up,
that we may live before him.
Let us know, let us press on to know the Lord;
his appearing is as sure as the dawn;
he will come to us like the showers,
like the spring rains that water the earth.
(Hosea 6:1–3)

We've all experienced natural consequences before, whether we stayed up too late and were very tired at school or work the next day, or we ate too many sweets and got sick. Natural consequences are the result of our own actions; they're the effect of a cause we chose. We call them natural because they don't need outside interference. They're just the way the world works. If we go outside in the rain, we will get wet. If we jump from too great a height, we will injure ourselves.

When the prophet Hosea says that God has torn and struck down, he is talking about the natural consequences of sin. Hosea attributes them to God, not because God has specifically punished the Israelites, but rather because God, the creator of all of nature, allows us to experience the consequences of our actions. It's one of the ways that we learn and grow.

But God also heals us of the wounds our actions cause. He cares for us and loves us despite our choices. If we focus our minds and our hearts on getting to know the Lord, we cannot fail. No matter how many chances we've missed or mistakes we've made in the past, he will always keep showing up and showing his face to us. He will always raise us back up.

Conversation Starters

- Can you remember a time when you experienced a natural consequence? What was it? Was it effective?
- Would you rather experience a natural consequence or a punishment? Why?

PRAYER

Dear Lord, thank you for always being willing to heal us. Thank you for being as sure as the dawn and the spring rains. Thank you for being the Someone we can always count on. Help us to know you more deeply and to love you better. Amen.

Saturday of the Fifth Week of Lent

Who is a God like you, pardoning iniquity
and passing over the transgression
of the remnant of your possession?
He does not retain his anger forever,
because he delights in showing clemency.
He will again have compassion upon us;
he will tread our iniquities under foot.
You will cast all our sins
into the depths of the sea.

(*Micah 7:18–19*)

Think about all the things you delight in, the many things that bring a smile to your face and joy to your heart. When we delight in something, we take pleasure in it; we enjoy it, and we want to experience it over and over again.

That's how God feels about showing mercy. He doesn't show mercy reluctantly. Rather, he delights in it and finds joy in it.

You are not a burden to the Lord. Your sin isn't a burden to the Lord. He doesn't just put up with you or tolerate you. He doesn't get annoyed at having to forgive you for the same things over and over again. There will never come a time when the Lord does not delight in showing you mercy. No matter how many times you sin or turn away from him, he remains the same.

Conversation Starters

- What do you delight in? What does that tell you about who you are?
- Why do you think that God delights in showing mercy? What does that tell you about who he is?

PRAYER

Dear Lord, thank you for who you are. Thank you for delighting in us. Thank you for loving us. Thank you for your mercy and your clemency. May we never take it for granted, and may we also know deep within us that we are loved and cherished by you. Amen.

Holy Week

Today we begin the most sacred week of the Catholic liturgical year: Holy Week. It is a week full of traditions and rituals, a time spent apart to walk with Jesus on his final days before the crucifixion. This week we'll be reading passages from the Mass for each day.

Weekly Memorization Verse

But he was wounded for our transgressions,
crushed for our iniquities;
upon him was the punishment that made us whole,
and by his bruises we are healed. (Isaiah 53:5)

Palm Sunday of the Lord's Passion

The next day the great crowd that had come to the festival heard that Jesus was coming to Jerusalem. So they took branches of palm trees and went out to meet him, shouting,
"Hosanna!
Blessed is the one who comes
in the name of the Lord
— the King of Israel!"
Jesus found a young donkey and sat on it; as it is written:
"Do not be afraid, daughter of Zion.
Look, your king is coming,
sitting on a donkey's colt!"
His disciples did not understand these things at first; but when Jesus was glorified, then they remembered that these things had been written of him and had been done to him. So the crowd that had been with him when he called Lazarus out of the tomb and raised him from the dead continued to testify. It was also because they heard that he had performed this sign that the crowd went to meet him. (John 12:12–18)

The crowd that met Jesus at the entrance to Jerusalem greeted him with cheers and shouts of joy. They came because they had heard stories of miracles, of healings, of casting out demons. They heard he raised Lazarus from the dead. They thought they knew who he was and who he would be for them.

How quickly the story changes. By the end of the week, many of these same people will stand in front of Pontius Pilate and demand Jesus' death. Jesus knew that. And still, he rode into the city. He heard the crowd, saw their adoring faces, and knew they would betray him. But still he looked on them with love. He does that for us, too. He knows our past, our present, and our future, and he loves us.

As we enter into Holy Week, we'll be walking with Jesus through his final moments before the cross. He knew what was about to happen and he accepted it willingly, not only for the cheering crowd on Palm Sunday, but also for us.

Conversation Starters

- What would it have been like to be in the crowd on Palm Sunday?
- What do you think Jesus' apostles were thinking and feeling on that first Palm Sunday?

PRAYER

Dear Jesus, thank you for loving us in every moment of our lives. Please forgive us for the times that we have betrayed your trust and your love. Help us this week to draw closer to you. Amen.

Monday of Holy Week

Here is my servant, whom I uphold,
my chosen, in whom my soul delights;
I have put my spirit upon him;
he will bring forth justice to the nations.
He will not cry or lift up his voice,
or make it heard in the street;
a bruised reed he will not break,
and a dimly burning wick he will not quench;
he will faithfully bring forth justice.
He will not grow faint or be crushed
until he has established justice in the earth;
and the coastlands wait for his teaching.
(Isaiah 42:1–4)

The prophet Isaiah speaks of justice. Sometimes people think of justice as the opposite of mercy, as though the two are opposed to one another. Yet Jesus is both merciful and just.

Justice is one of the four cardinal virtues. In justice, we give to God what is due to God and to other people what is due to them (what they deserve). God deserves love, praise, and obedience. We also deserve love and to have our dignity upheld, for we are made in God's image and likeness. But there are very real consequences for our sins, which harm our relationships with God and others.

Jesus came to earth to be both just and merciful. In dying for our sins on the cross, Jesus ensured that justice was served. At the same time, by taking on the punishment that rightly belonged to us, he was merciful.

God will not break a bruised reed or quench a dim light. God knows the weight of our sins would have done just that to us, so he chose to protect us, hold us, and bring us back to him. Because he loves us, he won't ever crush us.

Conversation Starters

- What do you think the word *justice* means? What comes to mind when you think of that word?
- How can mercy and justice work together?

PRAYER

Dear Jesus, thank you for loving us. Thank you for protecting us and shielding us. Thank you for being both merciful and just; help us to emulate you in both. Amen.

Tuesday of Holy Week

Now while Jesus was at Bethany in the house of Simon the leper, a woman came to him with an alabaster jar of very costly ointment, and she poured it on his head as he sat at the table. But when the disciples saw it, they were angry and said, "Why this waste? For this ointment could have been sold for a large sum, and the money given to the poor." But Jesus, aware of this, said to them, "Why do you trouble the woman? She has performed a good service for me. For you always have the poor with you, but you will not always have me. By pouring this ointment on my body she has prepared me for burial. Truly I tell you, wherever this good news is proclaimed in the whole world, what she has done will be told in remembrance of her." (Matthew 26:6–13)

The woman in this passage recognizes something that the apostles do not: Jesus is on his way to death. Her response might seem strange to us now, but back then pouring oil on someone showed that God had set that person apart for a special purpose. Priests, prophets, and kings in the Old Testament were all anointed with oil. The anointing is an outward sign that points to an inward reality. The woman's action showed the apostles an important truth: Jesus had a special purpose. He came to die for our sins.

As Catholics, we use holy oils in the sacraments of baptism, confirmation, anointing of the sick, and holy orders. During Holy Week, the bishops of each diocese consecrate the holy oils that will be used throughout the next year.

PRAYER

Dear Jesus, thank you for giving us tangible signs such as anointing with oils to help us remember truths that we might otherwise forget. Thank you for the witness of the woman who saw what your apostles didn't and responded to you in love. Amen.

Conversation Starters

- Have you ever seen a sacramental anointing? What did you notice? What do you remember?
- Why do you think the Church uses oil and other physical items to celebrate the sacraments?
- How do you think the apostles felt after Jesus told them that the woman's actions would be remembered wherever the Gospel was spread? Why?

Wednesday of Holy Week

Then one of the twelve, who was called Judas Iscariot, went to the chief priests and said, "What will you give me if I betray him to you?" They paid him thirty pieces of silver. And from that moment he began to look for an opportunity to betray him. (Matthew 26:14–16)

The Church calls today Spy Wednesday because this is the day when we read the story of Judas' betrayal of Jesus. It's easy for us to listen to the story and think, "I could never do that," but the reality is that every time we sin, we betray Jesus too.

Judas was one of Jesus' twelve apostles, chosen personally by the Lord out of all of his disciples. Just like the other apostles, Judas gave up everything in his life to follow Jesus. For three years he lived with Jesus, listened to Jesus, and was loved by Jesus.

But it wasn't enough. Judas betrayed Jesus for thirty pieces of silver.

The most heartbreaking part of the story comes later, though, when Judas realized he made a mistake. Heartbroken, Judas didn't go to Jesus with his pain. He didn't seek forgiveness or reconciliation. Judas gave in to the temptation to despair and believed the lie that he had done something unforgivable.

Today calls us to remember that no one is beyond redemption. No one is beyond saving. There is no sin too big for the Lord to forgive, no sin that is not covered by the cross. If Judas had run to Jesus, he would have heard that truth. Let's not make the same mistake. Let's always run to Jesus in our sins.

Conversation Starters

- Why do you think Judas decided to betray Jesus? What might have happened to lead him to make this choice?
- How do you think he felt after he was paid the thirty pieces of silver by the chief priests?

PRAYER

Dear Jesus, today we remember the moment that your chosen apostle betrayed you. Please forgive us for the times that we have sinned and betrayed your trust. Please help us to always return to you and ask for your mercy and forgiveness. Amen.

Holy Thursday

I am the true vine, and my Father is the vinegrower. He removes every branch in me that bears no fruit. Every branch that bears fruit he prunes to make it bear more fruit. You have already been cleansed by the word that I have spoken to you. Abide in me as I abide in you. Just as the branch cannot bear fruit by itself unless it abides in the vine, neither can you unless you abide in me. I am the vine, you are the branches. Those who abide in me and I in them bear much fruit, because apart from me you can do nothing.

Whoever does not abide in me is thrown away like a branch and withers; such branches are gathered, thrown into the fire, and burned. If you abide in me, and my words abide in you, ask for whatever you wish, and it will be done for you. My Father is glorified by this, that you bear much fruit and become my disciples. As the Father has loved me, so I have loved you; abide in my love. If you keep my commandments, you will abide in my love, just as I have kept my Father's commandments and abide in his love. (John 15:1–10)

Can you imagine a tree branch choosing to cut itself off from the tree? That wouldn't make much sense; would it? But that's what we do to ourselves when we walk away from Jesus. Like branches that get cut off from the tree, when we cut ourselves off from Jesus, we cut ourselves off from the source of our life.

Jesus is the vine. And just like the vine supplies nutrients and water to the branches, Jesus supplies us with grace through the sacraments. Just like branches on the vine, our job is to stay attached and receive. If we move away from him, if we cut ourselves off from his grace, we may not feel different for a while. But eventually, we will dry up and wither. We need him, and we can't live without him.

Conversation Starters

- What do you think would make someone cut themselves off from Jesus?
- What are some ways that you can stay rooted in him? How can we help you do that?

PRAYER

Dear Jesus, thank you for being the vine. Thank you for all the ways that you share your graces with us. Thank you for keeping us close to you. Help us to always remain in your love. Amen.

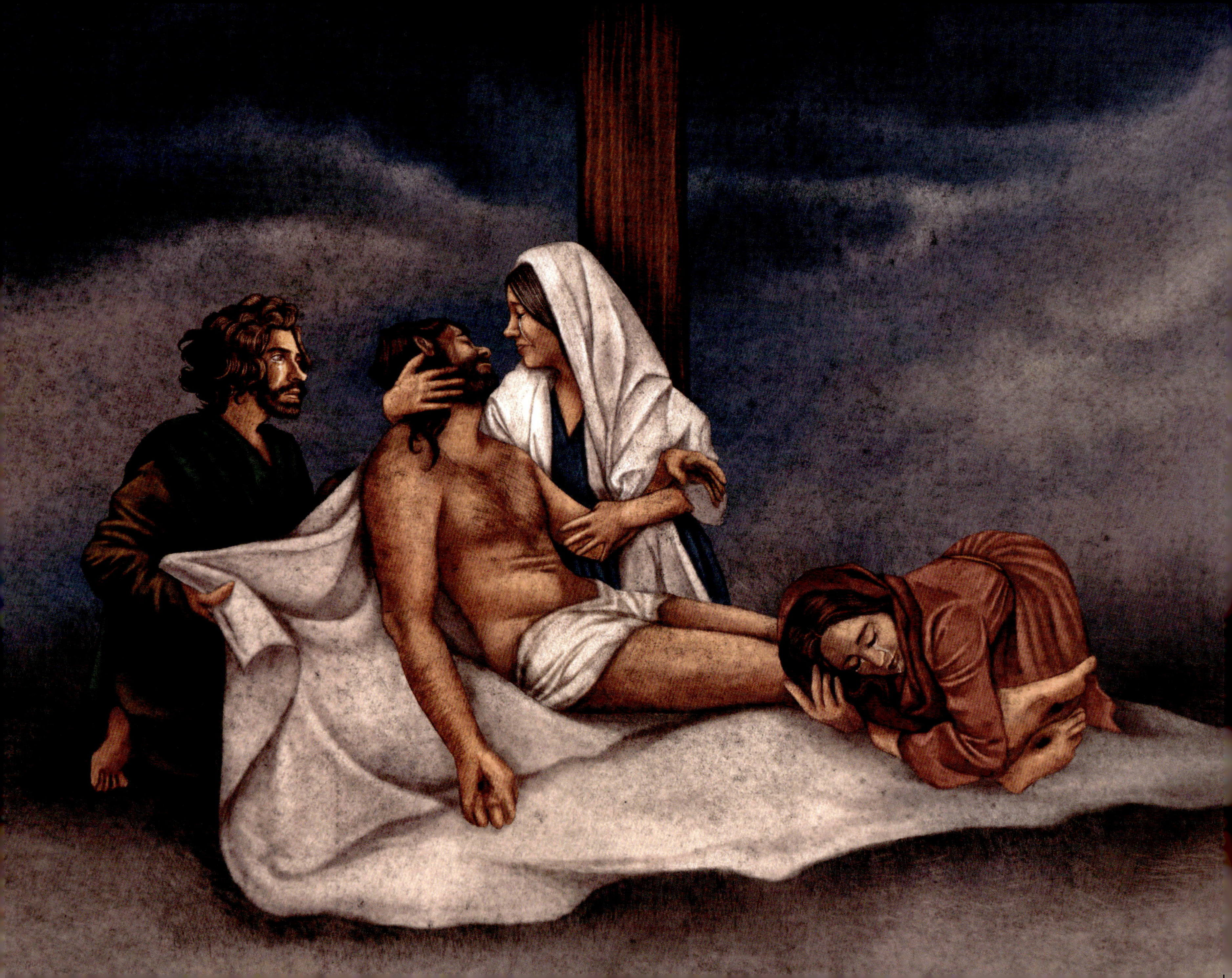

Good Friday

Surely he has borne our infirmities
and carried our diseases;
yet we accounted him stricken,
struck down by God, and afflicted.
But he was wounded for our transgressions,
crushed for our iniquities;
upon him was the punishment that made us whole,
and by his bruises we are healed.
All we like sheep have gone astray;
we have all turned to our own way,
and the LORD has laid on him
the iniquity of us all.
He was oppressed, and he was afflicted,
yet he did not open his mouth;
like a lamb that is led to the slaughter,
and like a sheep that before its shearers is silent,
so he did not open his mouth.
By a perversion of justice he was taken away.
Who could have imagined his future?
For he was cut off from the land of the living,
stricken for the transgression of my people.
They made his grave with the wicked
and his tomb with the rich,
although he had done no violence,
and there was no deceit in his mouth. (Isaiah 53:4–9)

Why is Good Friday good? It is a day when we remember the crucifixion, the most painful death a person in Jesus' time could have experienced. We mourn the death of Jesus. We fast, weep, and pray. And yet, we call it good.

Today is good because this is the day Jesus died for our sins. Without his death, we would have no hope of heaven. Without his death, we could not live eternally with God. Without his death, we would be stuck in our sin. Because he died for us, we can live. His death, though awful, saves us; and thus this day is very good.

Conversation Starters

- What do you feel when you think about what Jesus experienced for you today?
- Do you think it's right that we call this day "Good"? Why?

PRAYER

Dear Jesus, thank you for coming to suffer and die for us. Holy Spirit, help us to understand the depth of Jesus' sacrifice as we ponder it today. Amen.

Holy Saturday

Next day, that is, after the day of Preparation, the chief priests and the Pharisees gathered before Pilate and said, "Sir, we remember how that imposter said while he was still alive, 'After three days I will rise again.' Therefore command the tomb to be made secure until the third day; otherwise his disciples may go and steal him away, and tell the people, 'He has been raised from the dead,' and the last deception would be worse than the first." Pilate said to them, "You have a guard of soldiers; go, make it as secure as you can." So they went and made the tomb secure by sealing the stone. (Matthew 27:62–66)

If you walk into a church today, you'll notice a few important changes. The lights will be dim, if any are on at all. The red sanctuary lamp by the tabernacle will be extinguished, and in many parishes the door to the tabernacle will be wide open, revealing that the Eucharist is not there. It's a stark reminder that Jesus has died. You will not find him here.

But we know that Jesus is about to rise. As the guards at his tomb would soon discover, there was no stone big enough, no obstacle great enough to keep Jesus in the tomb. On Holy Saturday, we remember the time Jesus spent in the tomb. Yet in our churches, we also venerate the emptiness of the tabernacle because we know that it signifies what is to come.

Conversation Starters

- Have you ever been to a church on Holy Saturday? What did it feel like?
- How do you think the Pharisees felt when they watched the stone roll in front of the tomb? Why?

PRAYER

Dear Jesus, thank you for the silence of the tomb. Thank you for the emptiness of the tabernacle and the chance to ponder your death. Thank you also for the reality that nothing can keep you in the grave, and that tomorrow we will rejoice with you and celebrate your resurrection. Amen.

Introduction to the Octave of Easter

The resurrection of Jesus is too big of an event to celebrate in a single day. The Church, in her wisdom, gives us an entire octave (an eight-day period) to feast. Each day within the Octave of Easter is a solemnity, a mini-Easter. That means you can (and should) be celebrating throughout the week.

Throughout the Octave of Easter, we'll be reading passages from the Gospels that tell us what Jesus was doing on earth after his resurrection. We'll walk with the apostles and share in their joy (and sometimes confusion).

Weekly Memorization Verse

When it was evening on that day, the first day of the week, and the doors of the house where the disciples had met were locked for fear of the Jews, Jesus came and stood among them and said, "Peace be with you." After he said this, he showed them his hands and his side. Then the disciples rejoiced when they saw the Lord. (John 20:19–20)

Easter Sunday

After the sabbath, as the first day of the week was dawning, Mary Magdalene and the other Mary went to see the tomb. And suddenly there was a great earthquake; for an angel of the Lord, descending from heaven, came and rolled back the stone, and sat on it. His appearance was like lightning, and his clothing white as snow. For fear of him the guards shook and became like dead men. But the angel said to the women, "Do not be afraid; I know that you are looking for Jesus who was crucified. He is not here; for he has been raised, as he said. Come, see the place where he lay. Then go quickly and tell his disciples, 'He has been raised from the dead, and indeed he is going ahead of you to Galilee; there you will see him.' This is my message for you." So they left the tomb quickly with fear and great joy, and ran to tell his disciples. Suddenly Jesus met them and said, "Greetings!" And they came to him, took hold of his feet, and worshiped him. Then Jesus said to them, "Do not be afraid; go and tell my brothers to go to Galilee; there they will see me." While they were going, some of the guard went into the city and told the chief priests everything that had happened. (Matthew 28:1–11)

An angel appeared to the women at the tomb to announce the resurrection of Jesus. The angel offers the women a chance to see the empty tomb and then sends them on a mission to spread the Good News that Jesus is risen.

We are called to be like these women. We are meant to be witnesses to the truth that Jesus died for our sins and rose again. We are meant to be filled with joy and to share that joy with those around us.

As Catholics, we are an Easter people. We are called to live in the joy of the Resurrection. What can that look like in our lives today? What can that look like in our family?

Conversation Starters

- Why do you think the women didn't fall to the ground shaking when they saw the angel? How would you have reacted?
- Why do you think they felt fear as well as joy?
- What ways can you spread the joy of Easter?

PRAYER

Dear Lord, may the joy of the Resurrection permeate our souls and fill our hearts. Help us to spread your joy to those around us, and to share with them the Good News of the Gospel.

Easter Monday

Early on the first day of the week, while it was still dark, Mary Magdalene came to the tomb and saw that the stone had been removed from the tomb. So she ran and went to Simon Peter and the other disciple, the one whom Jesus loved, and said to them, "They have taken the Lord out of the tomb, and we do not know where they have laid him." Then Peter and the other disciple set out and went toward the tomb. The two were running together, but the other disciple outran Peter and reached the tomb first. He bent down to look in and saw the linen wrappings lying there, but he did not go in. Then Simon Peter came, following him, and went into the tomb. He saw the linen wrappings lying there, and the cloth that had been on Jesus' head, not lying with the linen wrappings but rolled up in a place by itself. Then the other disciple, who reached the tomb first, also went in, and he saw and believed; for as yet they did not understand the scripture, that he must rise from the dead. (John 20:1–9)

Peter and John run to the tomb after Mary Magdalene tells them that Jesus is risen. They find it empty and see the burial cloths lying there. But John, the narrator of this story, makes it clear that they didn't understand the Scripture. That's an astounding admission from one of Jesus' closest friends and trusted apostles.

John doesn't seem ashamed of his lack of understanding. He is humble; he knows who he is, he knows that Jesus loves him, and he knows it was OK that he didn't understand. Far from being ashamed of his lack of understanding, John chose to include it in his Gospel account. He could easily have left that detail out. But John knew the most important thing: He was loved by Jesus.

When we know that, nothing else matters. Our reputations, what people think of us, how we are perceived in the world — none of it can touch us if we know with every fiber of our being, as John did, that we are loved by Jesus.

Conversation Starters

- What do you think John and Peter expected to find in the tomb?
- How would you have responded to seeing the empty tomb?

PRAYERS

Dear Lord, please help us to know your love and ground our identity in it instead of in what other people think. Thank you for loving us so much. Amen.

Easter Tuesday

But Mary stood weeping outside the tomb. As she wept, she bent over to look into the tomb; and she saw two angels in white, sitting where the body of Jesus had been lying, one at the head and the other at the feet. They said to her, "Woman, why are you weeping?" She said to them, "They have taken away my Lord, and I do not know where they have laid him." When she had said this, she turned around and saw Jesus standing there, but she did not know that it was Jesus. Jesus said to her, "Woman, why are you weeping? Whom are you looking for?" Supposing him to be the gardener, she said to him, "Sir, if you have carried him away, tell me where you have laid him, and I will take him away." Jesus said to her, "Mary!" She turned and said to him in Hebrew, "Rabbouni!" (which means Teacher). Jesus said to her, "Do not hold on to me, for I have not yet ascended to the Father. But go to my brothers and say to them, 'I am ascending to my Father and your Father, to my God and your God.'" Mary Magdalene went and announced to the disciples, "I have seen the Lord"; and she told them that he had said these things to her. (John 20:11–18)

Have you ever heard anyone say your name with so much love that you could *feel* it? Can you pick out your mom or dad's voice in a crowd if they call your name?

This passage teaches us a little bit about resurrected bodies. Jesus doesn't look quite the same. Mary doesn't know him even though it is daytime, and they aren't far apart. Only when he says her name does she recognize him.

Sometimes in life, the Lord might not look or act as we expect. But his voice remains the same. We can keep close to the Lord by listening to his voice —in the form of Scripture, of the teaching authority of the Church (the Magisterium), and of our pastors, bishops, and the pope.

Conversation Starters

- Is there someone you care about whose voice you can recognize without seeing them? How do you feel when you hear their voice?
- What are some ways you can learn to hear God's voice in your heart?

PRAYER

Dear Jesus, help us to become more aware of your voice. Please fill us with your Holy Spirit so that we will thirst for your word and desire to know you more deeply. Amen.

Easter Wednesday

As they came near the village to which they were going, he walked ahead as if he were going on. But they urged him strongly, saying, "Stay with us, because it is almost evening and the day is now nearly over." So he went in to stay with them. When he was at the table with them, he took bread, blessed and broke it, and gave it to them. Then their eyes were opened, and they recognized him; and he vanished from their sight. They said to each other, "Were not our hearts burning within us while he was talking to us on the road, while he was opening the scriptures to us?" That same hour they got up and returned to Jerusalem; and they found the eleven and their companions gathered together. They were saying, "The Lord has risen indeed, and he has appeared to Simon!" Then they told what had happened on the road, and how he had been made known to them in the breaking of the bread. (Luke 24:28–35)

We don't know much about the two disciples on the road to Emmaus. In fact, we don't even know both of their names. What we do know is that they were leaving Jerusalem, even after they had heard the news of Jesus' resurrection. They could not believe. They did not understand. And so they left.

But like any good shepherd, Jesus isn't about to let his sheep wander off. He follows them. He rebukes them, yes, but he doesn't leave them in their confusion and unbelief. He walks with them and talks with them, patiently explaining what they didn't understand. And then he blesses the bread and offers them his very Body.

Jesus can handle it when we're confused by Church teaching, or when we don't understand something that we see happening in the world. He will meet us on our journey, but it's our responsibility to respond like the two disciples — by asking him to stay with us and listening when he speaks.

Conversation Starters

- What do you think the two disciples were saying when Jesus appeared to them?
- How do you think they felt when he disappeared?

PRAYER

Dear Jesus, may we always be disciples that stay close to you and your Church. And please, should we ever wander, come and find us and bring us home. Amen.

Easter Thursday

While they were talking about this, Jesus himself stood among them and said to them, "Peace be with you." They were startled and terrified, and thought that they were seeing a ghost. He said to them, "Why are you frightened, and why do doubts arise in your hearts? Look at my hands and my feet; see that it is I myself. Touch me and see; for a ghost does not have flesh and bones as you see that I have." And when he had said this, he showed them his hands and his feet. While in their joy they were disbelieving and still wondering, he said to them, "Have you anything here to eat?" They gave him a piece of broiled fish, and he took it and ate in their presence. (Luke 24:36–43)

"Touch me and see," Jesus says to the disciples. He invites them to do the very thing that he explicitly told Mary Magdalene not to do. At first glance, our response might be, "Hey, that's not fair." And it isn't. God doesn't ever promise us fairness. He doesn't ever promise to give us the same thing that he gives everyone else. He tells us that he will give us what we need, though. His grace is sufficient, and he will provide our daily bread.

Mary Magdalene didn't need to touch Jesus. She already believed. She knew the truth of the Resurrection and was ready to do the will of God. The disciples were still confused, however, so Jesus offered touch, giving them what they needed to move forward in faith.

Sometimes we might be tempted to look with envy at the gifts and blessings God gives someone else. Instead, let's follow the example of Mary Magdalene, who didn't cling to the Lord. She received the gift he gave her with joy and focused on what he asked of her, not what he was doing for others.

Conversation Starters

- Has there ever been a time when you felt you weren't being treated as well as someone else? How did that feel? What might have helped you in that moment?

PRAYER

Dear Lord, help us in those times when we are tempted to envy others for the gifts you give them. Remind us that you love us and see us as individuals and that you will provide for our needs. Amen.

Easter Friday

After these things Jesus showed himself again to the disciples by the Sea of Tiberias; and he showed himself in this way. Simon Peter said to them, "I am going fishing." They said to him, "We will go with you." They went out and got into the boat, but that night they caught nothing.

Just after daybreak, Jesus stood on the beach; but the disciples did not know that it was Jesus. Jesus said to them, "Children, you have no fish, have you?" They answered him, "No." He said to them, "Cast the net to the right side of the boat, and you will find some." So they cast it, and now they were not able to haul it in because there were so many fish. That disciple whom Jesus loved said to Peter, "It is the Lord!" When Simon Peter heard that it was the Lord, he put on some clothes, for he was naked, and jumped into the sea. But the other disciples came in the boat, dragging the net full of fish, for they were not far from the land, only about a hundred yards off. (John 21:1, 3–8)

Peter loved Jesus so much that he jumped into the sea to get to him. He couldn't even wait for the boat to bring him to shore.

Throughout much of the Gospels, Peter is impulsive. He says what he feels and acts on impulse, often without thinking first. Sometimes, it gets him in trouble, but not this time. Remember that Peter has just recently denied Jesus, that he stayed away from the crucifixion out of fear. But when he sees the Lord, he runs to him, not away like Judas did. He trusts in who Jesus is more than he is ashamed of what he has done.

PRAYER

Jesus, please grant us the grace to love you as much as Peter and to always run to you, even when we have sinned. Amen.

Conversation Starters

- What do you think the other apostles thought about Peter jumping into the water?
- What do you think you would have done if you had been Peter or one of the other apostles?

Easter Saturday

Now after he rose early on the first day of the week, he appeared first to Mary Magdalene, from whom he had cast out seven demons. She went out and told those who had been with him, while they were mourning and weeping. But when they heard that he was alive and had been seen by her, they would not believe it. After this he appeared in another form to two of them, as they were walking into the country. And they went back and told the rest, but they did not believe them. Later he appeared to the eleven themselves as they were sitting at the table; and he upbraided them for their lack of faith and stubbornness, because they had not believed those who saw him after he had risen. And he said to them, "Go into all the world and proclaim the good news to the whole creation." (Mark 16:9–15)

The apostles didn't believe in the Resurrection at first. They did not even trust the witness of others. And yet, they are the eleven men chosen by the Lord to proclaim the Gospel, to forgive sins, and to bring the Eucharist to the world.

Why? We do not know Jesus' mysterious reasons, but these are the men he chose. And this passage from Mark gives us a clear indication that he didn't choose them because they were perfect. It's worth remembering that we, like them, are not defined by our worst moments or our weaknesses. God isn't put off by our mistakes or our stubbornness (though he will call us out on it). He sees us for who we are — men and women made in the image and likeness of God.

Conversation Starters

- How do you think the apostles felt when Jesus upbraided them for their stubbornness?
- Do you think you would have believed the reports of Mary Magdalene and the disciples who met Jesus on the road to Emmaus? Why?

PRAYER

Jesus, help us to see ourselves and those around us with your eyes. Help us to remember that we aren't our weaknesses or sins, but rather that we are yours and we are loved.

Divine Mercy Sunday

And as he sat at dinner in the house, many tax collectors and sinners came and were sitting with him and his disciples. When the Pharisees saw this, they said to his disciples, "Why does your teacher eat with tax collectors and sinners?" But when he heard this, he said, "Those who are well have no need of a physician, but those who are sick. Go and learn what this means, 'I desire mercy, not sacrifice.' For I have come to call not the righteous but sinners." (Matthew 9:10–13)

In the early 1900s, Jesus appeared to a young Polish nun named Sr. Maria Faustina Kowalska. In her *Diary*, she recorded his words to her and his message of mercy for the world. Today, one week after Easter Sunday, we remember that just as blood and water flowed from Jesus' side on the cross, so now grace and mercy always flow from his heart for us.

PRAYER

Dear Jesus, thank you for your mercy. May we always take advantage of the graces you offer and always allow ourselves to be immersed in your mercy. Amen.

Conversation Starters

- Why do you think that Jesus wanted us to celebrate this feast every year? Why do you think he chose to appear to Saint Faustina?
- How do you feel when you think about the greatness of Jesus' mercy?

Solemnities that Can Fall During Lent

Solemnity of Saint Joseph (March 19)

Now the birth of Jesus the Messiah took place in this way. When his mother Mary had been engaged to Joseph, but before they lived together, she was found to be with child from the Holy Spirit. Her husband Joseph, being a righteous man and unwilling to expose her to public disgrace, planned to dismiss her quietly. But just when he had resolved to do this, an angel of the Lord appeared to him in a dream and said, "Joseph, son of David, do not be afraid to take Mary as your wife, for the child conceived in her is from the Holy Spirit. She will bear a son, and you are to name him Jesus, for he will save his people from their sins." All this took place to fulfill what had been spoken by the Lord through the prophet:

"Look, the virgin shall conceive and bear a son,
and they shall name him Emmanuel,"

which means, "God is with us." When Joseph awoke from sleep, he did as the angel of the Lord commanded him; he took her as his wife. (Matthew 1:18–24)

Saint Joseph was a man of faith. He recognized the Angel of the Lord and believed what was spoken to him without questioning. He listened and followed the Lord's will, even when he didn't know all the details and probably didn't understand everything he did know. Joseph took to heart the Lord's request that he love Mary and Jesus. We don't have a record of any words he spoke, but his actions clearly show the kind of man he was. In silence, he worked for, protected, and loved his wife and child.

What would it take for us to love that deeply and trust that fully? Can we follow Joseph's lead in our own lives?

Conversation Starters

- What do you think Joseph did first after waking up from his dream? Why?
- How do you think Joseph felt about being the earthly father of the Messiah?

PRAYER

Saint Joseph, please be with us today. Please pray that our faith might grow as strong as yours and that we might also take Jesus into our homes and our hearts, cherishing and loving him as you did. Amen.

Solemnity of the Annunciation (March 25)

In the sixth month the angel Gabriel was sent by God to a town in Galilee called Nazareth, to a virgin engaged to a man whose name was Joseph, of the house of David. The virgin's name was Mary. And he came to her and said, "Greetings, favored one! The Lord is with you." But she was much perplexed by his words and pondered what sort of greeting this might be. The angel said to her, "Do not be afraid, Mary, for you have found favor with God. And now, you will conceive in your womb and bear a son, and you will name him Jesus. He will be great, and will be called the Son of the Most High, and the Lord God will give to him the throne of his ancestor David. He will reign over the house of Jacob forever, and of his kingdom there will be no end." Mary said to the angel, "How can this be, since I am a virgin?" The angel said to her, "The Holy Spirit will come upon you, and the power of the Most High will overshadow you; therefore the child to be born will be holy; he will be called Son of God. And now, your relative Elizabeth in her old age has also conceived a son; and this is the sixth month for her who was said to be barren. For nothing will be impossible with God." Then Mary said, "Here am I, the servant of the Lord; let it be with me according to your word." Then the angel departed from her. (Luke 1:26–38)

It is no coincidence that the feast of the Annunciation often falls during the Lenten season. Mary's yes to Gabriel made the Incarnation possible, but her yes was not a one-time event. Mary said yes to the Lord many times over the years. She said yes to Simeon's prophecy about her baby boy. She said yes when she found Jesus in the Temple. She said yes when he left home to preach, teach, and heal. She said yes when she met him on the way of the cross and offered the comfort of her presence. She said yes at the foot of the cross when Jesus asked her to become the mother of the Church.

Conversation Starters

- Whom do you think Mary told first about the angel's visit? Why?
- How do you think Mary felt when she heard Gabriel's words?

PRAYER

Dear Jesus, thank you for the gift of your mother. Thank you for the ways that she loves us and leads us to you. Amen.

Notes for Parents

ASH WEDNESDAY

Welcome to Lent! Today's meditation touches on the reality that all of us are far from the Lord in one way or another. This reading provides a wonderful opportunity to gently guide your children into some self-reflection. Consider using the conversation starters to help you understand how your children see their relationship with God and then use that knowledge to have a conversation about how you see those areas affecting them. Make sure to pair your observations with words of hope and encouragement. You could share a story from your life that shows how you returned to God or conquered a sin or bad habit with his help.

I love this reading because it illustrates brilliantly that Lent is not an individual endeavor. God invites his people back as a community, and as a community, we are meant to experience the return. This attitude of "we're all in this together" can be especially helpful if you are trying to cultivate an atmosphere of encouragement and support among your children. Knowing that mine often struggle with this, I like to highlight this part of the passage.

THURSDAY AFTER ASH WEDNESDAY

Lent is full of wonderful opportunities to grow closer to the Lord, but it's also a time when we can be especially tempted to compare ourselves to others. As parents, we may look at the moms and dads around us (or on the internet) and see daily Mass attendance, parish Stations of the Cross, and intense sacrifices, and begin to worry that we aren't doing enough. But here's the truth: God does not care if your Lent looks like any other family's. He just wants you to enter in with your whole heart and do what you can. I hope that in reading this psalm, you are reminded that God is not concerned with whether our Lenten penance is outwardly impressive, or how it compares to someone else's. Rather, he is concerned that we are consistently turning to him with our whole selves.

FRIDAY AFTER ASH WEDNESDAY

Jesus doesn't pull any punches in this teaching on prayer. He is blunt in his condemnation of prayer practices that are done so that others will think better of us. While giving alms and praying are certainly good things, the truth is that we can do the right thing for the wrong reasons. Jesus wants more for us than that. Our prayer time is meant to grow our relationship with God, not to be a measuring stick by which we judge ourselves or others. Thanks to social media, much of our family's life can play out in the public sphere. It's important for us as parents to remember that most of the work we do in raising our kids is hidden work, known only to the Lord. Don't ever let yourself believe that it isn't valued or seen by him.

SATURDAY AFTER ASH WEDNESDAY

One of the things that I love about Scripture is how accessible it is to both the old and the young. I can have a conversation with my young children about not judging other kids based on the clothes they wear or their behavior at the park, and yet still be convicted myself by the very same passage. We all judge others, and all of us have space to grow in this area. I'd encourage you to be honest and authentic with your kids as you discuss this passage. When we as parents admit our struggles, we tell our kids that it's safe for them to do the same.

FIRST SUNDAY OF LENT

This same mindset shift can be helpful when discussing Church doctrine or practices with our kids and can move them from a law-based approach to God to a deeper relationship founded on love. It's much more likely that they will keep their faith and remain in the Church if they can understand that the *why* behind all the *whats* is love.

MONDAY OF THE FIRST WEEK OF LENT

There is a lot of meat to this passage from Matthew, and there are many ways it can be approached and discussed depending on the ages of the kids in your family.

I like this passage for use in a large family because it reminds my kids that there are lessons to be learned from even our youngest members. It can be a beautiful opening for a discussion on respecting and appreciating younger siblings they might find annoying and help them to see their brothers and sisters from a new perspective.

It's also a chance for me as a parent to show vulnerability. I have found it especially fruitful as my kids have gotten older to share that there have been (and will be) plenty of times when I needed to be reminded to trust God more. I never want my children to feel like they can't come to me when they are struggling or wrestling with their faith, and the only way that will be possible is to let them see that my faith is far from perfect. Being authentic and honest with our children (in a way that is healthy and age-appropriate) gives them permission to be authentic and honest with us.

TUESDAY OF THE FIRST WEEK OF LENT

Today's opening verse can provide an opportunity to talk with your children about how and why your family might look different from other families you know. Even if you are blessed to be surrounded by a strong community of Catholics, it is likely that you have discerned differently from those around you on one topic or another, whether that is in regard to technology use, dress and manners, or activities. In my family, this passage gives us an opening to talk about our values and to give our kids the *why* behind many of the choices we have made.

WEDNESDAY OF THE FIRST WEEK OF LENT

The idea of hungering and thirsting for God is found throughout both Scripture and the writings of the saints. Today's Scripture passage provides a wonderful opportunity for you to share a part of your personal testimony with your kids and describe a time when you felt a deep thirst for God. It's important that our kids know that we as parents have experienced this.

THURSDAY OF THE FIRST WEEK OF LENT

I love this passage because it is so flexible. There are as many ways to struggle with humility as there are people in the world. As a simple example, this particular passage speaks to two of my kids in very different ways.

My eldest son has a nervous system disability that is a big challenge for him. There are parts of daily life that he struggles with through no fault of his own. This passage is a reminder to him that he can lean on God's grace and strength when he's having a hard time. It tells him that he's not broken, that he is loved for all of who he is, and that he's not judged by his disability.

My eldest daughter struggles in the opposite way: She is always honest about her struggles, but she needs help remembering that her strengths are gifts and they are good. She has a tendency to make herself less, to sink into the background, and to downplay her talents to herself and others. This passage is an opening for her father and me to remind her that she was created in the image and likeness of God, and that he has bestowed great gifts on her. She should be proud of them!

As you discuss humility today, remember that humility is about identity. It's about seeing ourselves in relationship with God. Some of our kids are going to struggle to confront and admit weakness, whether that's a challenge inherent to them or a sinful habit. But others are going to struggle to remember that they are good, holy, incredible kids who are beloved by the Lord. As Catholic parents, we want them to be able to hold both of those things in tension because they have their eyes fixed on the Lord, and they know who he is.

FRIDAY OF THE FIRST WEEK OF LENT

Today is a great opportunity to talk with your kids about confession and to make a plan to go together sometime this Lent. According to the *Catechism of the Catholic Church*, all Catholics of an age to receive Communion should go to confession and receive the Sacrament of Reconciliation at least once a year. It's worth noting, too, that the Church teaches that we should not receive the Eucharist unless we are in a state of grace — that is, we haven't committed an unconfessed mortal sin.

Confession can be daunting, especially if you haven't been in a while, but Lent is the very best time to return to the practice. I've found it easiest to get to confession when our whole family goes together. My husband and I take turns: One of us watches the kids and the other receives the sacrament, and then we swap. Many parishes offer confession before the Saturday vigil, but most priests are willing to schedule confession time if you call the parish. This can be a great option for families. It's also worth checking to see if there is a local religious order that offers a different confession schedule. For example, the Capuchins here in Detroit offer confession every day of the week.

The *Catechism* has a section that touches on the Sacrament of Reconciliation and the nature of sin. Both are worth reading if you or your kids have questions.

SATURDAY OF THE FIRST WEEK OF LENT

This is one of my favorite passages in the Bible. I return to it often for myself and my kids. It speaks to our very identity as beloved children of the Father. One of the most important things to me as a mother is that my children know and understand this at the core of their beings. If they do, it will be so much more difficult for the world to tear them down or to tempt them to another path. Lent is a wonderful time to ground them in the Faith, and to remind them of their identity in the Lord.

SECOND SUNDAY OF LENT

Today's passage from Matthew is a wonderful opportunity to practice *lectio divina*, a type of prayer used within the Church for centuries. This method of prayer is a meditative reading of Scripture, which can include prayerful discussion with others and private journaling.

I encourage following this simple process when practicing *lectio* as a family, especially if you have young children:

- First, set the stage: Ensure that everyone is paying attention and is quiet and peaceful (or as peaceful as small children get).
- Next, tell the children that you are going to read from Scripture, and that this is one of the ways we learn to hear God's voice. Ask the children to pay attention to any words that stick out in their mind as they listen.
- Then, read the passage slowly and prayerfully. Make sure to pause after the first time you read the words and ask your children if they need any of the words explained to them.

- Spend a few moments in silence, and encourage your children to think about the word or words that stood out to them as you read.
- Then read the passage aloud one last time.

This way of reading and praying with Scriptures can be a game-changer in helping you share your faith with your children in a way that feels natural and easy for your family.

MONDAY OF THE SECOND WEEK OF LENT

There are so many different ways to model inviting God into our lives. One of the things that I have found most effective with my children is verbalizing my own prayers when my kids are in earshot. So if I'm about to pray in my heart or head, "Please, Lord, help me to be able to focus well on my work" or "Lord, thank you for this beautiful weather," I instead say it out loud. It was uncomfortable at first, but it has made a difference in the prayer lives of my kids, who now also pray out loud when they think of the Lord.

TUESDAY OF THE SECOND WEEK OF LENT

This passage is a reminder to me to constantly seek God's will in my own life but also to remember to ask the Holy Spirit to come to me and teach me how to pray for my kids. I'm their mom, so I know more about them than anyone else on this earth at this stage in their lives. And that means that sometimes I think I know exactly what they need and how God should move in a situation concerning them or our family. The reality is, though, I could be wrong. Even if I have the best of intentions, I might be praying for the wrong things. Asking God to help me understand his will, and truly seeking that out, has changed the way I pray for myself and others.

WEDNESDAY OF THE SECOND WEEK OF LENT

The last part of this passage can be a helpful opening for discussing sibling relationships, particularly those that are full of conflict. Sometimes we need to remind our kids that their brothers and sisters (or cousins or friends from school or the kids on the playground) are made in the image and likeness of God.

THURSDAY OF THE SECOND WEEK OF LENT

Today's Scripture passage from First Chronicles describes an event that happened early in the reign of King David, just after the

Ark of the Covenant had been brought to Jerusalem. The people were rejoicing, and David had this psalm sung aloud. It was a way to remind his people not to forget the God who had done so much for them now that they were out of danger.

Reading it feels as though King David is calling me out personally. The Lord has truly done so much for me in my life, yet I do not sing his praises nearly enough. I become forgetful in my prayer time, coast in my faith, and fail to be really present to God unless I need something from him.

Lent is a beautiful time for me as a mom to remember that not only do I need to lean into my everyday relationship with my Lord, but I also need to be more mindful of modeling that for my children.

FRIDAY OF THE SECOND WEEK OF LENT

At the beginning of the Book of Nehemiah, we learn that the survivors in Jerusalem are in great trouble and shame because they have no walls to protect them. Historically, having a wall around your city signaled importance and value. At this time, however, Jerusalem's walls had been torn down by enemies, and the city had been left open to attack. This was shameful to the inhabitants because they were vulnerable.

Nehemiah returned to Jerusalem, and, in the midst of incredible opposition, rebuilt the walls of the city. But his prayer in this passage serves as a spiritual wall around his people before he builds them a physical one. He knows that they are vulnerable, not just to attacks of armies but to the lure of pagan gods and a loss of trust in the Lord.

This passage reminds me that the prayers my husband and I pray for our children can be the walls they need to grow up in security and certainty in the love of God.

SATURDAY OF THE SECOND WEEK OF LENT

Psalm 66 provides a great opening for a conversation with our kids about the unconditional love of God. If your kids are older, today's reflection offers a wonderful opportunity to break open the complicated parts of King David. He's a prime example of true repentance as well as someone who kept turning to God even when he didn't get it right (which will tie in nicely with next week's theme of repentance).

THIRD SUNDAY OF LENT

Our choices, both good and bad, have consequences. We can't rest on our Catholic faith and not expect to be held accountable. That's the hard truth about this passage from Matthew that most of us would probably like to gloss over.

While it's important that we not spend more time than is due focusing on hell and the consequences of sin, as parents we are responsible for helping our children understand that sin does objectively damage their relationship with God and others — sometimes mortally.

These conversations don't have to be lengthy lectures or fire-and-brimstone style preaching (in fact, they'll probably go better if you don't use those methods). For my own children, we've found that the best way to encourage them to avoid sin is to focus on their personal relationship with Jesus. When they understand that hell is the absence of God for eternity, and they love God very much, they don't want to make choices that will send them there. That's a large part of why today's meditation focuses on not taking our relationship with God for granted.

MONDAY OF THE THIRD WEEK OF LENT

"For as the heavens are higher than the earth,
so are my ways higher than your ways
and my thoughts than your thoughts" (Is 55:9).

There is comfort in this passage if we are brave enough to admit that we don't know as much as we think we do. Yet this is hard, especially as parents. As our kids become older, we have to remember that we aren't in control of their choices, and we aren't in control of how God is going to move in their lives.

But there is also hope in that reality. I have found in my own life that too often my imagination is too small for the wonders that God is working in the lives of those I love. This passage from Isaiah reminds me not to put God in a box and to trust him when I don't understand how he's moving.

TUESDAY OF THE THIRD WEEK OF LENT

Repentance is a hard topic for kids, as most parents who have watched their kid struggle to apologize know. Confronting our own mistakes and taking accountability for our actions is something that most of us struggle with, even adults. Today is a great day to be honest with your kids (at an age-appropriate level) about any times in your life when you struggled to go to confession or make a change in your life even though you knew you needed to. This vulnerability helps our kids know that we are safe people to talk to and that we will understand instead of judging if and when they find themselves stuck in sin and struggling to get out down the road. It's also a good day to assess what preventive measures your family is taking regarding sin. What things are you doing regularly to prevent "spiritual cavities"?

WEDNESDAY OF THE THIRD WEEK OF LENT

As my kids get older and begin to see more of the world, I find that I rely on the wisdom of this passage more and more to help guide them through the gray (and sometimes black!) areas of popular culture. It's easy to fall back on a law-based understanding of good and bad, one that sorts people into predetermined groups based on the behavior we see in them. It's also easy to let the pendulum swing too far in the opposite direction and never call out any bad for fear of being judgmental or not "nice."

What Jesus asks the Pharisees to do in this passage he also asks of us as parents: to walk in the complicated middle ground of hating sin and loving sinners and teaching our kids to do the same. It's not easy, and it requires a great deal of discernment and prayer, but it is possible.

THURSDAY OF THE THIRD WEEK OF LENT

Today's reflection provides a great opening to talk with your children about the consequences of sin. There are many ways in which today's culture glorifies sin and makes it appear that actions don't have consequences. It's important to remind our kids that their eternal life matters, and that even if we don't see the effects of sin here on earth, we will at the end of our lives.

FRIDAY OF THE THIRD WEEK OF LENT

Any parents who have ever tried to teach their children a lesson in a roundabout way will empathize with the challenge that Baruch is facing in this Scripture passage. The people on whose behalf he is speaking are living in exile. They are far from the Lord both physically (the Temple has been destroyed, and they have been sent to other countries as refugees) and spiritually (many have fallen into false worship). While Baruch addresses himself to God, he is speaking indirectly to the Jewish people. By using this rhetorical technique, Baruch lessens the defensiveness of his people, making it more likely that his words will penetrate hearts. For me as a mom, Baruch is a reminder that sometimes it's more fruitful to approach a problem with my children sideways instead of head-on.

SATURDAY OF THE THIRD WEEK OF LENT

To help us learn about what it means to be merciful, the Church calls us to practice the of Works of Mercy, both corporal (bodily) and spiritual. By performing these works for one another, we grow in imitation of the mercy of God.

The Corporal Works of Mercy, which help people with their physical needs, are:

- Feed the hungry.

- Give drink to the thirsty.
- Shelter the homeless.
- Clothe the naked.
- Care for the sick.
- Visit the imprisoned.
- Bury the dead.

The Spiritual Works of Mercy, which help people with their spiritual needs, are:

- Instruct the ignorant.
- Counsel the doubtful.
- Admonish the sinner.
- Comfort the sorrowful.
- Forgive injuries.
- Bear wrongs patiently.
- Pray for the living and the dead.

The Corporal and Spiritual Works of Mercy are essential components of our Catholic faith. All of us are obligated to practice them according to our ability and station in life. We should be looking for ways to incorporate them more into our family's routine. Perhaps we can't participate in prison ministry, but it might be within our ability to visit someone homebound due to age or illness. Perhaps we don't have a room to spare for someone in need, but we can support the local homeless shelter in our area.

I encourage you today to brainstorm ways that your family can make practicing the Works of Mercy a priority. Include your kids in the brainstorming process!

WEEK FOUR INTRODUCTION

This week's Scriptures focus on our relationship with God. It's worth noting here that forgiveness and reconciliation are two separate things, though the words are often used interchangeably. We must understand the difference because it can vastly change the way we see our obligations to ourselves and others. Teaching our children the difference will also help them to have healthy relationships. Forgiveness requires one person: the party who was wronged. We are obliged to forgive those who hurt us. Reconciliation requires two people: both the person who was injured and the person who did the injuring. We are all obliged to forgive, but we are not necessarily obliged to be reconciled with people who have hurt us. This is an important distinction to make, both within ourselves and for our children. Reconciliation with God is always possible, and is always the right choice. Reconciliation with other human beings is more complicated.

FOURTH SUNDAY OF LENT

Saint Thérèse of Lisieux is often admired for her humility, but what strikes me most every time I pick up her autobiography (*Story of a Soul*) is her audacity. It's something that I strive to emulate and want very much to pass on to my children. In one passage, she talks about running to God the Father in the moment after her sin and failure. She would picture herself as a little girl and climb right up onto the lap of her loving Father, asking him for mercy and love instead of punishment. At first glance, this seems fanciful and flowery. But pause and think about it for just a moment and you can't fail to notice the almost shocking level of trust and faith she has. To run to God in the exact moment she realizes she has sinned? How many of us have lost that childlike trust and have had it replaced with a deep feeling of unworthiness and fear of punishment? Let's ask Thérèse to intercede for us that we might remember what it feels like to have childlike faith, and that we might help our children to retain theirs as well.

MONDAY OF THE FOURTH WEEK OF LENT

One of the best ways that we as parents can help our children understand the importance of this lesson from Matthew is by modeling apologies. My husband is exceptional at this, and I'm learning to be better at it myself. We both consciously try to make sure that we are apologizing to each other in front of our kids and to them when necessary. It's already bearing fruit in our children's lives, both in the way they approach one another and the way they understand the Sacrament of Reconciliation.

Oftentimes society tells us that admitting fault makes us appear weak or lessens our authority, but it actually does the opposite: It shows our children that we are confident enough and courageous enough to admit our mistakes. It sends them the message that these words of Jesus hold weight in our everyday lives and should in theirs, too.

TUESDAY OF THE FOURTH WEEK OF LENT

Adults often underestimate what children are capable of. But when we do give them responsibility and show them that we believe they are able to fulfill it, most of the time they do. I'd encourage you to help your children, no matter how young, realize that Saint Paul is speaking to them in this passage. They are ambassadors for Christ by virtue of their baptism into his Church.

They can show others the power of reconciliation. Let that empower them. Younger children can be reminded that they can do this through the kindness and love they show others. Older children can be reminded that ambassadors are often the first representatives people meet and can make either a good impression or a bad one. What are they showing the people in their lives about what it means to be Catholic?

WEDNESDAY OF THE FOURTH WEEK OF LENT

Some people would argue that passages like this one from Colossians are not suitable for children, or that the message will simply go over young kids' heads. But it's important to begin to teach our children, no matter how young they are, that they are part of the Body of Christ and full-fledged members of God's family.

Depending on your child's age, this passage might not spark a lot of discussion today, but it will bear fruit in their lives down the road.

If we want them to be able to understand it later, to apply the truth of this passage in their lives, then we need to expose them to it now. Even if we do not understand a passage of Scripture when we first encounter it, or even the second or third time we read it, it can stick in our heads and help form our hearts, which means that we are ready to receive its truth when we need it.

THURSDAY OF THE FOURTH WEEK OF LENT

When I was a young adult, I served for a time as a missionary, and we prayed the Liturgy of Hours — also called the Divine Office — three times a day. The prayers each day are largely comprised of psalms and canticles, which are prayed in a four-week cycle. Since we prayed the Divine Office regularly for a few months, we prayed the same psalms over and over again. Pretty soon, I had most of them memorized. They became part of me, and to this day, the passages from those psalms are often the first words that spring from my lips without conscious thought or effort in times of trial.

Today's verse for memorization is one that I want my kids to know deeply. I want them to understand that God their Father will run to them and meet them when they are at their lowest. I want that desperately because I know how prevalent are the temptations of the world in which they are growing up.

FRIDAY OF THE FOURTH WEEK OF LENT

A quick note today on the specifics of the conflict that Saint Paul is speaking about in this letter to the Church in Ephesus. As Christianity spread geographically, it was also spreading across cultures, which meant clashes were happening, specifically between Jews and Gentiles. The Jewish people marked their covenant with God by circumcision. It was a physical sign of a spiritual reality. It set them apart from other people. But with the coming of Jesus, that covenant was expanded, and Saint Paul wanted to make sure that both Jews and Gentiles realized that they are all one (and equal) in Christ.

SATURDAY OF THE FOURTH WEEK OF LENT

Today is another opportunity to share with your kids an experience that you have had with the Sacrament of Reconciliation. Can you share with them a time when you felt God's love through confession? Or what it feels like to you when you hear the priest say the words of absolution?

WEEK FIVE INTRODUCTION

While many of the previous weeks have focused on the ways we need to return to the Lord, this week will focus on the actions of God himself more than our own. This is hugely helpful for children who are older and may be struggling with allowing themselves to be loved for who they are. This week's passages will remind them (and us) that they are loved fully and unconditionally by the Lord.

FIFTH SUNDAY OF LENT

This passage from Zephaniah is part of a larger prophecy, and it's helpful to know some of the context of that prophecy in order to understand it better. Zephaniah is one of the twelve minor prophets of the Old Testament, and according to Saint Jerome, his name meant "watchman of the Lord."

Zephaniah prophesied in Jerusalem to the people of Judah. After the death of King Solomon (the son of David), the Kingdom of Israel was split in two: Ten of the twelve tribes of Israel rejected Solomon's heir and became the Kingdom of Israel. The remaining two tribes stayed with the Davidic line and became the Kingdom of Judah. On the whole, the Kingdom of Judah was more faithful to God during this period than the Kingdom of Israel, though both still faltered and sinned greatly.

Zephaniah's prophecies were focused on the Kingdom of Judah, and though he was bold and even blunt in calling out their sinful behavior as a nation, he was also confident in the Lord's ability to renew and restore his people. It's an important nuance that we shouldn't lose sight of as parents.

MONDAY OF THE FIFTH WEEK OF LENT

Ezekiel is one of the four major prophets of the Old Testament. A member of the upper class, he lived during the Babylonian exile and was the first prophet to speak to God's people who were living outside of Israel or Judah. By this time, the Temple in

Jerusalem, the pride and joy of the Israelite people, had already been destroyed. And yet, Ezekiel spoke of hope to the Israelite people in exile, to those longing to return to their homeland.

This passage is a great blockade against cynicism. Most of us have places within us that are cold, wounded, or walled off from God. Do we truly believe that God can do for us all that he claims in this passage? Do we live out that truth so our children will believe it and live from it as well?

A note on this passage: When Ezekiel spoke of being ashamed, he was not shaming the Israelites but calling them to repentance. And when he told them to be humbled, he used the word in its truest sense: True humility comes when we remember both who the Lord is and who we are in relationship with him.

TUESDAY OF THE FIFTH WEEK OF LENT

My eldest daughter is highly empathetic, which means she sees others and understands what they're experiencing. But it also means that she (like me) tends to take on more responsibility than she is meant for. If she knows I'm having a challenging day, she'll try to parent her younger siblings to give me a break. When we're at Mass, she'll try to be the one to distract the squirming toddler or the about-to-tantrum four-year-old.

While we love that she cares for others, my husband and I are quick to remind her that she isn't a parent. It's not because we don't want her to help or to love her siblings or care about what's going on around her. But we want to make sure that she's on the right side of the fine line between helping others and losing herself. (During Mass, for instance, when she's trying to distract a sibling, it means she's missing the prayers or Scripture, when God might be hoping to speak to her heart through them.) If this is something that you've ever struggled with, I'm right there with you; and today is a great day to open up to your children about a time when you either took on too much or when you had the confidence and strength to say no to a burden that wasn't yours.

WEDNESDAY OF THE FIFTH WEEK OF LENT

There's an old saying that every sinner is the same, but every saint is unique. One of my favorite things about Catholicism is that it is a big tent: There are as many ways to love God and live out our vocations as there are people on the earth. Today's Scripture passage provides an opening to speak with your children about their own calling and remind them not to compare themselves to others. It would be a beautiful day to share with them a bit of your story about discovering your own vocation.

THURSDAY OF THE FIFTH WEEK OF LENT

As its name suggests, this letter from Saint Paul was written to an individual rather than an entire community. Titus was a Gentile and a trusted assistant of Paul. He traveled with Paul on several of his journeys and, at the time of this letter's writing, had been sent to Crete, an island that Paul had never visited, where he was charged with developing the Church.

Even though he had never been to Crete, Paul certainly knew (or at least could guess) the challenges that Titus would face. And while there is plenty of practical and administrative advice in the letter, it's also clear that Paul wanted to make certain that, above all else, Titus knew whose he was and how he was loved. As parents, sometimes we can get stuck in the weeds of life. We can be bogged down with very real, and often urgent, material needs — which means we can forget to remind our kids how much God loves them, how richly he pours out his grace upon them, how much he desires to renew and restore all that is broken in their lives.

FRIDAY OF THE FIFTH WEEK OF LENT

I love natural consequences as a parent. They are incredibly effective — that is, provided I keep myself from stepping in and stopping my kids from experiencing them. There are times when it's difficult to let my kids suffer or fail, but it's easier when I take a long view: when I remember that my goal for them is heaven, and that human beings do, in fact, learn better through experiences. It helps to know that God uses them, too, and it helps to know that I can follow his lead in always being there to heal and bind up in love after.

As an aside, if you haven't read the whole Book of Hosea, I highly recommend it. It's a beautiful love story — the tale of a God who loves his people dearly despite how unfaithful they are to him.

SATURDAY OF THE FIFTH WEEK OF LENT

The prophet Micah, along with the book of the Bible that bears his name, is one of the more obscure prophets. He was a contemporary of Isaiah and lived in the eighth century BC. Though he is counted as one of the twelve minor prophets, he was on the fringes even during his lifetime. An outsider from the foothills of Judea, Micah was not popular with the wealthy and powerful. He preached strongly against corruption, but his prophecies were not all doom and gloom. It was Micah who foretold that Bethlehem would be the birthplace of the coming Savior (see Mi 5:2).

The passage today is one of my favorites from Micah because it shows us two things: first, that God *delights*, which is itself a revelation of the identity of God; and second, that he delights in showing clemency. I can't imagine he wouldn't also be delighted if we showed more of it ourselves.

HOLY WEEK INTRODUCTION

The Church offers many traditions that we can observe during Holy Week. I'd encourage you to give some of them a try, especially if you've never experienced the liturgies of the Triduum. But if you're in a difficult season of life, know that it's also OK to do as much or as little as you are able. God will still pour out his graces. Your family can still lean into this week if you aren't able to attend any parish events, and I encourage you to continue to use the daily reflections in this book as a jumping-off point for your prayer and discussion.

PALM SUNDAY OF THE LORD'S PASSION

Though most commonly known as Palm Sunday, the official name for today's feast is "Palm Sunday of the Passion of the Lord." At Mass today you'll hear two Gospel readings, one before the processional hymn and one in its normal place after the second reading. The reflection passage offered in this book comes from the first Gospel reading from Mass. The second Gospel reading at Mass today is the Passion of the Lord. The Church in her wisdom gives us both on this day, allowing us to reflect on the beginning and the end of the week together.

A liturgical fun fact: This year's palms will become next year's ashes.

MONDAY OF HOLY WEEK

Today's verse for memorization is one of my favorites in Scripture. I have taken comfort in its truth more times than I can count. It's one that I turn to often in my motherhood, particularly in seasons that feel too stressful or too busy, or in which there are too many needs that must be met. This verse reminds me of the truth that God will not crush me or allow me to be crushed. It reminds me of his presence and protection in times of trial. I memorized this verse as a young woman in my twenties, and I remain so grateful for it today. I didn't realize then how valuable it would be to me now, but it stands as a powerful reminder to me of why memorizing Scripture is so important. I hope that you find that to be true for you as well.

TUESDAY OF HOLY WEEK

The three holy oils consecrated at the Chrism Mass each year are the Oil of the Sick (used during the anointing of the sick), the Oil of Catechumens (used during baptism), and the Sacred Chrism (used during baptism, confirmation, and holy orders). The Sacred Chrism is unique in that it is olive oil mixed with balsam, which gives it a distinct smell. This oil signifies the presence of and sealing with the Holy Spirit.

After the Chrism Mass, the oils are brought back to each parish, where they will be processed to the altar on Holy Thursday during the Mass of the Lord's Supper. Afterward, they'll be kept in an ambry, a cabinet, usually made of wood and glass, affixed to a wall in the church. Often, the ambry is near the baptismal font. This year, look for your church's ambry and point it out to your kids. Or, if your children are younger, invite them to search for it and show you where it is!

WEDNESDAY OF HOLY WEEK

Today is a heavy day. The betrayal of Judas is a reminder of our own failures and how even those who are most devoted to their faith can be pulled away from God if they are not careful.

Sadly, Judas' story ends in suicide, a tragic ending that could have been avoided if he had run to Jesus after his betrayal. It's a hard topic to discuss with kids, but it is worth being honest about, as is appropriate for your children's ages and maturity levels. We always remind our children that Peter's betrayal was forgiven because Peter repented. There is no sin, no betrayal, no harm that the Lord cannot forgive and heal if we will only trust him enough to ask.

INTRODUCTION TO THE TRIDUUM

This evening the Church enters into the Triduum. *Triduum* is a Latin word that means three days, and this time is marked by three special liturgies that occur only once a year. Each day in this Notes for Parents section, I'll share some traditions that the Church holds and information about each of these liturgies.

I encourage you to check with your parish about when they will celebrate these liturgies, and to take part if you can. In our family, we have found these are three days each year worth breaking our schedules for. But if you are in a difficult season or unable to change your schedule due to work or other obligations, please know that while God offers us much grace in these liturgies, you are not required to attend. The only obligation is to attend Mass on Easter Sunday. The important thing is to find a way to live into these days for yourself and with your family, even if it's from home. The daily reflections that follow are meant to help you do this.

HOLY THURSDAY

Depending on the ages of your children, this day is perfect for discussing the choices, both big and small, that we make to remain with the Lord. *Abide* is an action verb. It is a verb that shows agency, a verb that requires choice — in fact, many choices — over the course of our lives. Many things in our lives will try to call us and our children away from Jesus, from the stress of current events, to discord within our families, problems with our friends, and the everyday stressors of life. But if we choose to abide with Jesus, we are guaranteed to bear fruit. Today's reflection provides a good opening for you to share a story from your own life about a time when you chose to abide in the Lord and offer tips to your children about what practices and habits help you stay with him.

Tonight's liturgy is the Mass of the Lord's Supper. Today's Mass is a special one, in which we will commemorate not only the Last Supper of the Lord, but also the institution of the priesthood. At Mass, your pastor will likely perform a ritual of washing the feet of parishioners, modeling Jesus' actions before the Last Supper.

After Mass, you'll be invited to process to the Altar of Repose. This is a special altar set up somewhere on the church grounds, where adoration will be offered for a time. This reminds us of Jesus' request that his apostles watch and pray with him in the Garden of Gethsemane. At the end of adoration, the Eucharist will be transported to a tabernacle in a private location. The tabernacle in the Church will remain empty until the Easter Vigil.

GOOD FRIDAY

The meditation today comes from Isaiah. Written centuries before the birth of Christ, it foreshadows the suffering that Jesus would take on. If you have younger children, they might need help understanding some of the words or images in the passage. If you have older children, this passage is particularly rich in imagery and fruitful for *lectio divina*.

A note about the Good Friday Liturgy: Today's Liturgy is not a Mass. There are many parts that will look like a Mass, and you will have the opportunity to receive Communion, but there will be no consecration of the Eucharist (on Holy Thursday, the priest consecrates enough hosts to last his parish until Easter). There are only two sacraments that are allowed to be celebrated on Good Friday: the anointing of the sick and reconciliation.

The liturgy will look very different today. Here are a few key components:

- After processing to the front of the church, the priests and deacons will prostrate themselves on the floor and pray in silence. This represents the grief and sorrow of the Church.
- The Liturgy of the Word will include the entirety of the Passion narrative.
- Today the Church will pray Solemn Intercessions, comprised of three parts: the intention, an opportunity for silent prayer, and a prayer said by the priest. These are often sung and include times of both kneeling and standing.
- After the Intercessions, a large cross will be brought into the sanctuary and held in front of the altar. The priest will venerate the cross, offering a bow and a kiss. He will then invite the parish to do the same.
- After the adoration of the cross, the priest or deacon will put on a humeral veil (a special garment used while carrying the Eucharist) and retrieve the ciborium containing consecrated Hosts. Communion will be offered, and after the service, the remaining hosts will be taken to a place outside of the church.
- At the end of the liturgy, the altar will be stripped bare, and all will depart in silence.

The Good Friday Liturgy is beautiful, and if your family can attend, you should consider it. That being said, a prayerful home recitation of the Stations of the Cross is also appropriate and suitable.

HOLY SATURDAY

Traditionally, Holy Saturday is a quiet day within the Church. We wait, we watch, we ponder. Obviously, depending on the ages of your children, the level of quiet you experience is going to be relative. Still, there are many ways to mark the day and set it apart. For example, our children usually enjoy TV on Saturday mornings, but on Holy Saturday, we fast from screen time.

OCTAVE OF EASTER INTRODUCTION

"We are an Easter people, and Alleluia is our Song." So said Pope St. John Paul II. The Church celebrates Easter for a full eight days, from Easter Sunday until Divine Mercy Sunday one week later. The Octave of Easter is a time to lean into the feasting and celebrating of the season even more deeply than we leaned into prayer and penance during Lent. I encourage you to find ways to help your children experience the full season of Easter, which will be celebrated until Pentecost, but especially the Octave.

The celebrations don't have to be elaborate, but it's so worthwhile to come up with concrete activities that can show your children that this feast of Easter is too important to be contained in a single day. My kids know that we have dessert every night during the Easter Octave and that I'm fairly free with the jelly beans too. I'll play praise and worship music, and because we homeschool, they'll get less work that week and more time to play. In little and big ways, we celebrate the Risen Christ.

A quick note on the Gospel passages we will reflect on during the Easter Octave: Each of the Gospel writers wrote slightly different accounts of what happened when Christ rose from the grave. It's worth exploring each of them with your kids, but for this devotional, I've tried to choose some that fit together in a cohesive narrative.

EASTER SUNDAY

Happy Easter! Each of the four Gospel writers has a different account of Jesus' resurrection on Easter Sunday. This account from Matthew is probably the most dramatic of the four, but it's wonderful to read each of them (not all today — remember that Easter is a longer season than Lent, so there will be plenty of time in the weeks ahead!). Because Scripture is the Living Word of God, you'll find that you and your children will each be struck by different parts of the story. It can be a wonderful opportunity to open up a discussion about what you each noticed and why.

EASTER MONDAY

Humility is at the heart of today's reading. John tells us that he doesn't understand something and permits us to not understand things, too. As parents, we often want to have all the answers, but there will always be times when we don't. It's important for us to be honest and authentic with our kids in those moments, just as John is with us, his readers.

EASTER TUESDAY

Names are powerful, and so is the way we speak them. As parents, we can show our children that they are known and loved in the way we speak to them. Do we say their names in love? Do we look for things to praise and proactively choose to see and speak the good in them? Or do we speak their names more often in annoyance or frustration? I'll admit that sometimes I find I do. In those moments, this passage reminds me of the power of a name, of a voice full of love. In those moments, I pray to be more like the Lord.

EASTER WEDNESDAY

Jesus loves your children. He loves them in their confusion and their questioning. He loves them when they walk away from him and when they don't believe. But he will never leave them. He will never leave us, either. Let that truth sink into you, especially if you have a child who has started down a different path than you had hoped. Keep praying and trust that Jesus is present.

EASTER THURSDAY

Today's meditation was inspired by my eldest son, who, several years ago, wondered at the unfairness of Jesus telling Mary not to touch him when he let Thomas probe his wounds. Answering him, I used examples from his own life and the lives of his siblings — times when we parented them differently but still loved them the same amount. This passage is a good reminder that we shouldn't always strive for *equality* or sameness; more often than not, what we need is *equity*.

EASTER FRIDAY

Today is a "meat Friday," which means the normal Catholic penance of abstaining from meat on Friday is removed because it's Easter. My kids love "meat Fridays," and they've come to associate them with special feasts — which is, of course, exactly what we want.

A note for Catholics in the United States: In 1966, the U.S. bishops made abstaining from meat on Fridays an optional practice except during the Lenten season, but Catholics are still highly encouraged to abstain from meat on Friday as a way of marking Friday as a penitential day throughout the year. If abstaining from meat is not possible, the bishops recommend substituting a different sacrificial practice in its place. My own family began abstaining from meat on Fridays all year long many years ago, and it has been a fruitful practice for us.

EASTER SATURDAY

As you can see from this passage, Mark's Gospel is the most succinct of the four. He goes into less detail than the other writers about what Jesus did and said, but he gets his point across. As we come to the end of the Easter Octave, I hope that you'll continue journeying with the Risen Lord throughout the full forty days of Easter, using the four Gospels as a guide.

DIVINE MERCY SUNDAY

The feast of Divine Mercy, occurring yearly on the Second Sunday of Easter, was instituted by Pope St. John Paul II in 2000 during Saint Faustina's canonization Mass. It's a poignant day to end a devotional, not least because, by its very nature, it draws us closer to Christ.

Jesus told Saint Faustina, "I desire that the Feast of Mercy be a refuge and shelter for all souls, and especially for poor sinners. On that day the very depths of my tender mercy are open. I pour out a whole ocean of graces upon those souls who approach the fount of my mercy. The soul that will go to Confession and receive Holy Communion shall obtain complete forgiveness of sins and punishment. On that day, all the divine floodgates through which grace flow are opened. Let no soul fear to draw near to Me, even though its sin be as scarlet" (*Diary* 699).

In Saint Faustina's diary, I have found countless passages for meditation, discussion, and growth. And now that my daughter is reaching an age to understand them, it has provided me with a new avenue to walk alongside her as she grows in her faith. In the Chaplet of Divine Mercy, I've found a set of prayers that are engaging to my children, who seem drawn to the Mercy of Christ the way most children are. If you have never prayed it, I highly encourage you to learn the Divine Mercy Chaplet. You can find the prayers at usccb.org/prayers/chaplet-divine-mercy or thedivinemercy.org/message/devotions/pray-the-chaplet.

SOLEMNITIES THAT FALL DURING LENT

Solemnity of Saint Joseph

The feast of Saint Joseph is a solemnity, which means it is a feast of the greatest importance in the liturgical year. Celebrated on March 19, it always falls during the season of Lent, though because Easter is a movable feast, its placement during the Lenten season changes each year. As a solemnity, the feast of Saint Joseph takes precedence over the penance and fasting of Lent. If

March 19 falls on a Friday, Catholics are allowed to eat meat that day.

Solemnity of the Annunciation

St. Louis de Montfort taught that when we say "Mary!" in prayer, Mary says, "Jesus!" We can be assured that Mary always and only ever leads people closer to her Son. She is Queen of Heaven and the quickest way to his heart. If your family is struggling to find your footing with regard to a prayer rhythm or ritual, or if you're looking to deepen what you already have, I highly recommend a devotion to Mary (or a consecration to her).

About the Author

Colleen Pressprich is a former missionary and former Montessori teacher turned homeschooling mom who strives to use the lessons she learned in the mission field and the classroom to live her dream of growing the domestic church. She is the author of several books, including *Marian Consecration for Families with Young Children*, *The Women Doctors of the Church*, *The Jesse Tree for Families*, *OSV Kids Rosary*, *OSV Kids Discover: The Pope*, and *Real Moms of Real Saints*. She lives with her husband, children, and mom in Michigan, where she loves everything about spring, summer, and fall, and absolutely hates the winter.

ABOUT THE ILLUSTRATOR

Amy Heyse is a Catholic artist who lives in Fort Collins, Colorado, with her husband, two daughters, and cat. Her favorite way to connect to God is through creating, and she loves to make artwork inspired by her prayer life. She has worked as a painting instructor for the past ten years and enjoys teaching artists of all ages. When she's not working on art, she loves watching movies and reading while snuggled up in her favorite bathrobe. You can learn more about her work at amyheyse.com.